Sa
Saying No

By the same author

Open Heart, Open Hands

Saying Yes, Saying No

John Glass

Collins

Marshall Pickering

First published in Great Britain in 1990 by Marshall Pickering

Marshall Pickering is an imprint of the Collins Religious Division, part of the Collins Publishing Group, 8 Grafton Street, London W1X 3LA

British Library Cataloguing in Publication Data

Glass, John
Saying yes, saying no.
1. Christian church. Pastoral work. Counselling
I. Title
253.5

ISBN 0-551-01972-7

Text set in 10/12pt Times by Avocet Robinson, Buckingham
Printed in Great Britain by Cox & Wyman Ltd, Reading

To my Parents

Contents

1: The Safest Place in the Universe

In my previous book *Open Heart – Open Hands* I investigated the importance of a life surrendered in total openness to God. Only those who make themselves vulnerable can be truly strong. Only those abandoned to the constraints of God's will, whatever He might demand of them, can really experience what divine guidance means.

Vital though openness certainly is, any one who has checked the security of their home prior to retiring for the night knows that doors are for closing too. Vulnerability to God's influence upon our total personality is the pathway to personal security only in so far as it is linked to a willingness to lock out those things that negate our continual growth and progress.

The Christian, when made aware of the Keys of the Kingdom, usually has a perception of them as being instruments of God's authority to open, release or to enter hitherto occupied territory. Often they are. Yet the child of God also has been given the power to use such keys in another way. Keys are also for closing.

In Genesis chapter 4 God graphically described sin to Cain as a creature that was 'crouching at his door, desiring to have him'.

Understanding those areas in which we are vulnerable to attack, and being willing to close them off once we are aware of them, is one of the most positive steps that the Christian can make to his own spiritual well-being.

Openness to God and being closed to the Enemy are two sides of the same coin.

Perhaps the greatest need of men and women is the need for security: physically, emotionally and spiritually. The Scriptures declare that, 'The Name of the Lord (all that He is and all that He represents) is a strong tower; the righteous run to it and are safe.'[1] Yet strongholds are not just places to run to: they are primarily command centres to fight from. Security is not only essential to a sense of subjective well-being, it is also vital to any attempt to bring help and ministry to the life of others. Two people floundering in a quicksand are likely, if trying to hold on to one another, to accelerate their own demise: to be sucked deeper faster. If, however, one is standing on the bedrock of solid ground, that individual is able, from their secure vantage point, to be the means of salvation to their sinking friend.

In the past twenty years the Christian Church has witnessed the ascending priority given to counselling; something brought about both by a continual disintegration of a society reeling under the body-blows administered by a world that condones immorality and embraces amorality, and an overdue restoration of its own approach to listening, caring and concern. Yet this welcome change has not been without its pitfalls.

It is possible that the counsellor, walking with their client through the narrow and painful labyrinths of hitherto private pain, can lose their vital sense of objectivity. Transference, that seductive psychological device in which the counselee idealises the counsellor as the perfect companion, partner or lover topples the consultant. The helper is rendered helpless and shares the quagmire with the victim. It would be a great mistake to assume that this minefield is only the preserve of an untrained lay person. Pastors and professional counsellors are particularly vulnerable – a fact highlighted by a recent survey conducted by the research department of *Christianity Today* among almost one thousand ministers. It would seem that when cracks appear in the ground beneath the 'rescuer' himself his options for falling are severely limited unless he too has someone to whom he is in a trusting relationship. For, as one of those who responded to the survey wrote, 'I would not dare tell a fellow minister my problems in this area. My denomination would forgive murder, but not impurity of thought'.

It becomes clear that the need for a personal security system – for keys that can turn both ways – to lock as well as open, is not just the responsibility of those who are normally considered to be vulnerable. Nobody is immune from the earth tremors that can so easily undermine a person's 'standing' in the Lord. Those who disagree might well consider the words, 'Let anyone who thinks he stands – who feels sure that he has a steadfast mind and is standing firm – take heed lest he fall into sin.'[2] God is able to keep us from falling if we let Him and this book is devoted to exploring and explaining the part that we can play in our own deliverance.

Wide Wings

When the Creation narrative is commenced in the opening verses of Genesis chapter 1 there is almost a tendency to skip over the second verse without noticing it. The problem is that it is sandwiched between two vital statements. The first proclaims, 'In the beginning God . . .' – important not only as the opening statement of the account given by Moses of the origin of the Universe but, even more significantly, the opening lines of the unveiling of all God's manifold purposes and design for humankind throughout scriptural revelation. It should never be forgotten that 'Revelation' is not only the name of the final book: it is the mandate of the whole Bible.

The other side of the second verse announces God's first recorded words in space and time, 'Let there be light'. Little wonder then that the second verse is viewed so often in the shadow of the other two. Poor relation though it is not. Although young David was left in the fields – overlooked while his brothers were looked over – yet he emerged later in his own right and rose to a stature that belied his initial impact. So this verse when brought from the twilight zone stands as tall as any other of the great foundations of the creative act:

> Now the earth was formless and empty, darkness was over the surface of the deep, and the Spirit of God was hovering over the waters.

The picture is of a great parent bird encompassing the whole Earth within the wingspan of its embrace and setting the right temperature and atmosphere for a million miraculous acts that would ensue wherever its shadow fell. Readers of the Authorised Version will notice the word 'brooding' in their translation – the incubating action of a fowl prior to the hatching of an egg. It speaks of the Spirit of God enveloping formless, dark and empty elements and, by His Presence, creating an environment conducive to the formation of a Creation perfect in structure and reason and with a beauty that no one on our side of the Fall has ever seen. One commentator puts it like this, 'God, with fostering care, calls forth the latent possibilities of a nascent world.'

This truth has a power that exalts it far beyond its application to the physical world. Its real impetus is seen as it hurtles, meteor-like, through history transcending the tangible and breaking through into things spiritual.

Every child of God experiences the Spirit's brooding in that pre-natal period prior to being born again. A person may have lived long with sin and guilt, shame and fear, anxiety and despair, emptiness and brokenness and then – from the middle distance – the Divine Eagle descends and hovers. Things begin to change. Belief begins to bud. Faith begins to rise. During this period of incubation every one of those previously insurmountable life-problems seem solvable by God. Nothing seems so large that it would fall outside His shadow. God can forgive me. He does love me. He did die for me. The egg begins to crack – new life springs forth. Once again, over the formless and the void, the Spirit's brooding has brought into being a new creation. This surely is what the chorus writer meant when he penned, 'Something beautiful, something good. All my confusion He understood. All I had to offer Him was brokenness and strife – yet He made something beautiful of my life.'

If this was true anywhere in space and time it was especially pertinent at that watershed of Christian experience, the Day of Pentecost. Day after day they prayed. Hour after hour they waited. One wonders, if they ended up with one hundred and twenty, how many they started with. How many gave up after a couple of weeks of hanging on to the promise of a new power? Tarrying takes time. Yet there the tenacious ones were when the Spirit descended and hovered over the upper room. Peter was present – the one who had denied Him with his words – but so were the other disciples who had denied Him by the conspicuousness of their absence, having previously all 'forsaken Him and fled'.[3] Not too many good self-images were on display. There was no form to follow and they were void of any excuses – what more perfect flight path for the Eagle. Their very emptiness lit up His runway. The windows rattled with the wind as He swooped. As the Spirit hovered over the house tongues of fire hovered over the occupants. Hearts were broken open and He who had 'brooded over' now came to dwell within.

Now when a Spirit-filled Peter strolled down the street those upon whom *His* shadow fell received creative acts of miracles in their lives. Why was this? The same Spirit that brought Creation into being and the same Spirit that raised Christ from the dead was now dwelling in them and, according to Romans 8 verse 11, was present to give life to mortal bodies.

The overshadowing of Omnipotence is also revealed in God's protective custody of His children. The heresy of Gnosticism, incorporating as it did within its tenets the worship of angels, rightly drew fire from the writings of the Apostle Paul as he tendered warnings to the Early Church. In consequence, contemporary Christians tend to treat with an understandable unease any tendency to bring angels into the limelight. Their role as ministering spirits is deemed to be very much as that of a 'supporting cast' if they are not relegated to the back stage altogether, behind the footlights, not listed among the cast. Yet 'behind the scenes' they are. The angel of the Lord encamps around those that fear Him. Only eternity will reveal what calamities would have befallen so many of us were it not for God's preventative and restraining grace administered by His supernatural sidesmen.

A number of years ago a senior missionary was required to transfer a sum of money personally from one mission station to another. He was to travel alone and to camp overnight in a desolate area that was notorious for the presence of bandits. Just at this time, thousands of miles away, a small church prayer meeting was in progress. Only sixteen people were present and during the time of intercession the group felt strongly the need to pray urgently for this man though, at that time, they did not understand why. The missionary completed his short expedition without any particular difficulty.

Several weeks later he was conducting an evangelistic crusade and at the end of the service, when many had responded to the call to salvation, a rough looking man stepped out from amongst those who had made a decision and approached the missionary personally. The man identified himself as a leader of a bandit gang who lived in the hills. He related how, a few months earlier, he and his men had heard news that a sum of money was to be transferred between two of the mission stations. He went on to say how they had followed the missionary and watched him camp overnight and how they had planned to return in the hours before dawn to kill him and steal the money. He spoke of returning to the location of the tent and being amazed to see it surrounded by sixteen armed soldiers and how they had withdrawn in bewilderment.

On furlough the missionary recounted the story in each church that he visited. His itinerary eventually brought him to the church where the sixteen people had been gathered in prayer months earlier. As diaries were checked and time-zones considered it was discovered that the presence of the sixteen armed soldiers corresponded exactly with the time that the local congregation had been engaged in prevailing prayer.

The ninety-first psalm puts it this way, 'He will command His angels concerning you to guard you in all your ways' – and the promise is followed by the vital qualification – 'If you make the Most High your dwelling.'

This is yet another example of the Spirit's brooding

for in the first verse we are told, 'He who dwells in the shelter of the Most High will rest in the shadow of the Almighty . . . He will cover you with His feathers and under His wings you will find refuge.'

There is far more than an echo of these words when Jesus, looking over the City of God cries, 'O Jerusalem, Jerusalem . . . How often I have longed to gather your children together, as a hen gathers her chicks under her wings, but you were not willing.'[4]

When the President of the United States initiated SDI (Strategic Defense Initiative), the intention of his 'Star Wars' programme was to create a technological panoply that would shelter America from the threat of galactic attack. For those whose trust is in the Lord His very shadow is become an impregnable shield.

There is protective care too at those times that the believer is engaged in what is euphemistically called the 'leap of faith'. Little eaglets do not instinctively fly from the nest to forage for food themselves. They are content to lie back in their downy home as the parent birds wear themselves out hunting on their behalf. The day comes however when the parent eagles have other things in mind for them. They want their young to learn to fly – yet who would expect an infant bird naturally to leap from dizzy heights into the unknown with untried wings with only their parent's promise that all will be well? Knowing this, the mature eagles set about removing the soft lining of the nest making their offspring's life so uncomfortable that leaping from their previously ideal habitat is nothing less than blessed relief.

Some of the tiny birds, as they launch themselves clumsily into what seems to them a great ocean of emptiness, begin to fly as soon as their wings begin to flutter. Others do not. Instead they fall, feather over beak, towards the valley's rocky floor. It is at this point that the parent eagles put the next phase of their plan into action. Swooping down with grace and speed they catch their tumbling offspring on their ample wingspan and bear it home on their back to the safety of the nest to try again. Deuteronomy 32 puts it this way:

> He shielded him and cared for him; He guarded him as the apple of His eye, like an eagle that stirs up its nest and hovers over its young, that spreads its wings to catch them and carries them on its pinions.

The literal Hebrew for 'brooding' and 'hovering' in Genesis 1:2 means to 'flutter loving' – a perfect picture of God's watching brief. Faith, however great the leap, can never be a kamikaze mission when initiated by the Father and executed within the hovering wingspan of His caring concern.

Strong Walls

I have never been a keen reader of spy thrillers or an avid watcher of films of a similar ilk. There is no doubt about it though; espionage is an industry almost as old as time itself and accounts of secret agents are not absent even from the Scriptures themselves.

Having been an agent once himself Joshua was well familiar with the military value of espionage. It is not surprising therefore that when he came against the strategic city of Jericho the first thing that he did was to send in men to reconnoitre the area.

Spies, if we are to believe the image that is presented of them, are something less than conventional creatures. Even so, by any standards, the fact that they took up residence in the house of a prostitute for the night[5] must have raised both questions and eyebrows when they reported back the results of their mission.

The fact is that not too many options were open to them. Private homes were out of the question. Inns were no alternative either. Their presence as foreigners within the walled city would have made them all the more conspicuous had they not sought out the privacy and anonymity of the harlot's house. It was vital that they take up lodgings in a place where it would not be unusual to see strangers both entering and leaving.

By the end of the story one of the securest cities imaginable is reduced to ruins and one of the weakest and most vulnerable inhabitants of it is preserved totally from harm and danger. Rahab must have possessed at least one key that kept her safe; in fact she had several.

1 The Key of Faith

We need to a have clear picture in our mind of exactly what the walls of Jericho looked like if we are to appreciate the full force of the story. If we conjure up a picture in our minds of the stone sides of a castle or even the types of wall that surrounds the Roman cities of York or Chester we will not be helped. Archaeologists inform us that the walls of Jericho were so thick that it was not uncommon to have chariot races along the top of them. The biblical account leaves us in no doubt that they were at least wide enough to embrace a whole house.

Once those that had come in pursuit of the spies had been sent off in the wrong direction, and before the secret agents had managed to settle down for the night, Rahab came to their sleeping quarters. There is nothing at all unusual about this scenario thus far, the woman's occupation being what it was. She was visiting them however in order to find out more about their God.

The following conversation between the three of them

allows us an insight into the faith of this remarkable woman. What we discover as we eavesdrop is the reason why the Holy Spirit, when inspiring the writer of the book of Hebrews to catalogue the greatest people of faith since the beginning of recorded time, includes her in the Sovereign's Honours List.

When she informed the spies that she knew that God had given them the land she probably exercised a great deal more faith than they had themselves at that moment in time. Everything they had seen thus far had only served to accentuate the virtually impregnable strength of the city that they had been sent to reconnoitre.

This evidence of faith was based not on any personal experience that she had with God or anything that she had witnessed for herself. It was founded only on reports that she had heard and miracles, such as the crossing of the Red Sea, that had been reported to her.

Twentieth-century 'believers' with the advantage of a full canon of scriptural revelation, the testimony of two thousand years of church history and a personal experience with God are still left with something to learn from her. Were it possible to take the words of Jesus to Thomas and project them back through time rather than forward they would surely refer to Rahab: 'Blessed are those who have not seen and yet have believed'.[6]

2 The Key of Appropriated Grace

It is one thing to believe that God is a powerful God. It is quite another to assume that He is willing to exercise His power on our behalf rather than against us. There is no doubt about it: Rahab had not clocked up many morality points towards earning favour from God – even if such favour could be earned. When she asked for protection and salvation from the coming calamity on the city many would have considered her request to be unbelievable presumption. She for her part saw it as an a natural response to a God who, if He was as mighty as He was reported to be, may be as great in grace as He was in power.

Having sought to solicit God's grace she then set out to test His generosity. She did not ask for salvation solely for herself but also for her father and mother, brothers and sisters and 'all who belonged to her'. When it comes to faith one wonders if had her name not appeared in the list in Hebrews 11, it would at least have qualified for the *Guinness Book of Records*. I sometimes wonder if it was Rahab that Newton the hymnwriter was thinking about when he wrote:

> Thou art coming to a King,
> Large petitions with thee bring.
> For His grace and power are such;
> None can ever ask too much.

3 The Key of Unquestioning Obedience

It is evident from the narrative that the spies, though perhaps shocked by Rahab's request, agreed to what she asked on the understanding that certain conditions were complied with. They needed a sign that would seal her faith. Looking around they saw a scarlet cord – a colour readily to hand given the woman's occupation – and told her to hang it outside the window if she expected to be saved. It would have been totally impossible for Rahab to see any logic whatsoever in the act, yet she complied with their instruction. Day after day, in the period between the secret agents' departure and the collapse of the city she would notice the scarlet strand. Its hue would remind her of two things. It was both a symbol of her sin and the seal of her salvation.

What a story for preachers of the Gospel. What a parallel there is between this and the account of the Passover.

The head of the family who had used hyssop as a brush to apply the blood to the doorposts forty years earlier would have seen far more in the symbolic act than ever Rahab recognised. To them the scarlet mark upon the lintel had clear associations with the sacrificial lamb from whence the blood had come. For them the shedding of blood had become both a covering and a means of salvation.

Such symbolism would have been too much for Rahab to understand, but she was obedient just the same. Fortunately, one does not have to understand the physics of electricity to turn on a light or the intricacies of soteriology to experience salvation.

There was another condition too. If she was to be delivered then she must be in a prescribed place when the judgement fell. To be living even a cubit outside the designated limits would have spelled disaster for her. If her relatives were also to be saved they were required to abide by the same rule. One may have thought that Rahab's house would, under normal circumstances, have been at the epicentre of any impending judgement. These were not normal circumstances. Like a later 'woman at the well' and 'thief on the cross', Rahab was to learn that even the hottest of brands can be plucked from the burning – even when milliseconds away from melting. If suspending the scarlet thread from her window was an act that possessed no logical significance, the request to call the people she loved most into a house built into a wall, with an earthquake on the way, called for more faith than many could muster.

The generation to whom Noah preached would have

thought that the ark was as likely to float as someone in the nineteenth century would have believed that a Boeing 747 could fly. Things like that had never happened before. Noah had no more scientific inside knowledge than his contemporaries possessed. The difference was that He had heard from God and believed what he had heard.

When Noah looked at the Ark he saw a sanctuary. When the people looked at it they saw a sepulchre. It was the place that God had designated for salvation and that was enough for him.

The generation to which he spoke saw things in a totally different light. If Noah was right and judgement was imminent, who wanted to spend their last hours in a floating farmyard – especially when there were grave doubts that floating was even a possibility? Noah had to make a choice. He chose the God he knew rather than the physics he didn't know. Both Noah and Rahab had learned to trust God rather than their limited understanding and both of them convinced their families to trust in God for salvation.

To many the cross is no more than a place of execution; a token of death. To the Christian it is the symbol both of life and salvation. The Apostle John, more than any other, speaks of abiding in Christ and making Him our sanctuary. As he does so he uses the greek word *meno* which means to 'remain and continue in'.

This is no more graphically illustrated than in the fifteenth chapter of his gospel when he records the teaching of Jesus with regard to the union of Himself and His followers.

> Remain in me and I will remain in you. No branch can bear fruit by itself; it must remain in the vine. Neither can you bear fruit unless you remain in Me . . . If you

> remain in Me and My words remain in you, ask whatever you wish, and it will be given you . . . As the Father has loved Me, so have I loved you. Now remain in My love.[7]

The union of branch and vine is central to an understanding of God's relationship with the believer. Those who are yet 'outside of Christ', and who claim to believe in the possibility of His existence, see His covering solely in terms of an air-raid shelter. He is someone to run to in trouble but to leave as soon as the 'all clear' has been sounded. Communion and relationship with God are often viewed by them as negative restrictions rather than positive blessings. Holiness is not understood as a secure sanctuary but as 'house arrest' – with all the concept of limitation of movement that goes with it.

Most of the scriptural symbols that signify the relationship of Christ with His Church are intimate ones: stones set in a building, members of a body, bridegroom in love with his bride.

The old negro spiritual that asked, 'O sinner man, where will you run to on that day?' highlighted an important principle of sanctuary. Though eleventh-hour conversions sometimes occur, they are not the norm.

'Grafting in' is the prerogative of the Gardener and the Bible tells us clearly of His identity. The initiative lies with Him, as no one can come to Christ except the Father draw him.[8] Vine life is the vehicle for Divine life. Everything that we have in Christ flows out of relationship, be it wisdom, insight, power, spiritual growth or answers to prayer. The teaching of Jesus in John 15 makes that clear.

The reason for this is that God longs to offer us more than just sanctuary. He wants to grant us sonship. Though in Old Testament times this aspect of continuing and intimate relationship could not be explored to the same extent that it can be experienced today, the Psalmist realised at least something of the importance of it. David was very security conscious even though, at times, he did not heed his own advice. He writes: 'He brought me up also out of an horrible pit, out of the miry clay, and set my feet upon a rock, and established my goings.'[9]

The last phrase literally means 'He steadies me as I go along'. The words could be used of a father hovering over an infant that totters as it learns to walk, catching and correcting the child as it stumbles.

God did not leave Rahab in the rubble-strewn remains of Jericho. He took her on a journey from degradation to dignity. She moved from being a prostitute to the position of princess. She became the great-great-grandmother of David and consequently her name is mentioned in the opening chapter of the New Testament as part of the genealogy of Jesus.

If ever there was a person in history who moved from tottering insecurity to the safest place in the universe it was Rahab. Many a man and woman has made a similar journey since.

2: Closing the Door on the Past

Inflationary pressures being what they are, the only good thing that can be said about 'living in the past' is that it was cheaper. That might be true economically but, spiritually, taking up residence in yesterday can often exact a heavy rent from the tenant.

There is a sense in which an understanding and appreciation of the past is not only important but essential. If a person wakes up in a hospital ward after a car accident and asks, 'Where am I?' they will not be satisfied simply with a response that defines their present location. The context is only comprehensible at the point that the events leading up to their current demise are able to be clarified.

When God called out to Adam in the Garden 'Where are you?'[1] He, The Omniscient One, was hardly wanting to elicit the response, 'Behind a tree'. Even fallen Adam knew that. 'I was afraid, because I was naked, so I hid' was a reply that stated, 'I am here because of where I have just been'.

Similarly, when God calls for Elijah He finds him, not hiding behind a tree on this occasion, but slumped wearily beneath its shade. The question, 'What are you doing here?'[2] evokes the explanation of the circumstances that have led up to his near-suicidal depression.

The past has an importance in that our current spiritual position before God is the end product of our walk thus far. If we are lost then thinking backwards to the place we diverted from our course is the first step to getting on the right road again. 'Thinking backwards' in order that I may approach the future more intelligently is both good and healthy. Living, and taking up permanent residence in yesterday, though, is a dead-end street: a cul-de-sac from which no one can ever grow or develop. Flowing streams are a haven for living things. Stagnant pools breed only disease.

There is a value in retrospection at the point that it becomes part of a learning process. For many years I have kept in my desk a small book in which I have scribbled notes to myself. The jottings evolve from a variety of situations. Perhaps I have conducted an interview with someone who finds themselves in a stressful situation. What is written down makes reference neither to the person nor the problem. The subject matter deals only with a review of my approach. Could I have been more sensitive. Did I listen sufficiently? I had at first only intended the exercise to last for the earlier part of my ministry. The notebook still remains.

For many people however the past has become both a predator and a parasite. A predator in that its threatening presence hovers over every current decision: a parasite in that its attendance sucks strength from all future endeavour.

The Spectre of Failure

Before Elijah ever met the widow of Zarephath God had told the woman that the prophet was on his way and would be requiring a meal from her.[3] She would not have heard the news gladly: and for two reasons. The first becomes immediately obvious as the account of the meeting is read. The woman was impoverished to the point that she could offer only a cup of water; the last morsel had gone from her larder and there was famine in the land. The second reason does not become apparent until the sequel of the story is reached.

She and her son possessed only a handful of flour and a little oil. It had been designated by them as their last supper; and they had resigned themselves to a slow death that they were certain was about to ensue. In obedience to the Lord however she surrendered what she had and found, like millions in generations that would follow, that it is impossible to outgive God.

For many the story ends there. What sacrificial faith. What total trust. If only we, like her, had such a reliance on God's faithfulness. Superficially all was well. Another miracle had been clocked up. To all intents and purposes the woman had entered a period of fulfilment and blessing from which she would never look back. All however was not as it seemed. On the surface her spirituality may have gained a radiant glow but inside her lurked an untreated bacteria that was about to break out.

The prophet had continued to lodge at the woman's house and after a while the widow's son became ill. At first it seemed there was nothing to worry about but he grew worse until eventually he stopped breathing altogether. She called upon Elijah for another miracle but the form of her request indicated that she too had need to join the healing line. 'What have you against me, man of God? Did you come to remind me of my sin and kill my son?' (The Scripture does not find it necessary to enlighten us as to the nature of her past transgression: it tells us only that she had sinned.)

When she first heard a word from God that a prophet was on the way to her home her immediate reaction would have been that he was coming to prophesy *against* her. It was inconceivable that God was coming to bless rather than to punish. Even the miracle of provision that she had experienced had not been sufficient evidence of God's caring concern. Her eyes saw the mounting burden of proof but the biased jury in her mind screamed out 'Guilty!' There had to be a catch. The death of her son suggested that there was.

As she blamed herself, Elijah blamed God. Both were wrong. When the young woman received the warm weight of her living child into her arms she had more than her son restored to her. She had lived through a famine and her relationship with God had been as barren as the fields around which she had been attempting to scratch a living. Now God had watered her. Flowers were beginning to grow. Forgiveness had begun to bud. God had not sent Elijah to her for the prophet's benefit. It was evident to her now that the appointment had been set up for her sake. She had been at the point of physical starvation and God had shown concern. Although what she had to eat mattered to Him, the thing that was eating her mattered to Him more.

Aristotle quoting Agathon who lived 400 years BC wrote, 'Even God cannot change the past'. Yet God in Christ has done so. He alters not its course once it has gone, but the judgement that it demands of us in the future.

Christ died for sins that are past.[4] That is what made Gethsemane so gruelling. When one man dies outside of Christ he faces an eternal hell. When Jesus took upon Himself the punishment for the sins of the world He paid the price of hells multiplied by the factor of the total population of humanity.

Before Calvary the blood of bulls and goats covered sin for a time. The sacrifice in the Old Testament period was simply a cover note that would be redeemed by the shedding of the blood of God's Lamb at a day that would be yet hence.

'God presented Him as a sacrifice of atonement, through faith in His blood. He did this to demonstrate His justice, because in His forbearance he had left the sins committed beforehand unpunished – He did it to demonstrate His justice at the present time, so as to be just and the one who justifies the man who has faith in Jesus.'

More than one mortal martyr has gone to the stake unflinching – in the anticipation of the destruction of their human body. Jesus sweated as it were great drops of blood in the hours before the cross for He, unlike them, was to atone for every sin that had ever been committed in the past as well as for every transgression that was yet to come.

Christ does not imprison the past as if it were a snarling and ravenous beast, telling us that it is now locked away behind closed doors and can no longer do us harm. Instead He faces death, destroys death and slays the beast. He then takes us by the hand and invites us to inspect its den and floods its lair with light. The victory of the cross has robbed the scorpion of its sting and the viper of its venom.

Past failure is not to be locked away in the hope that its presence will never come to light. Failure is to be faced. Once faced and repented of, like a cancer with no organ to invade, it withers and it dies.

The door must not be closed on sin prematurely. As repentance begins with a person agreeing with God about their sin, so forgiveness begins with the individual agreeing with God about its solution. Some find it far easier to agree with God about the former than the latter. They can believe that God has forgiven yet find themselves unable to forgive themselves.

It is said that long after the Edict of Emancipation that abolished slavery had been signed, negroes in the United

States were occasionally discovered working on farms in the same horrendous conditions. Well-meaning people showed them copies of the liberating document but to some it made little difference. Slavery was all they knew; especially if they had been born into it. Legally they had no need to serve the old master and, deceitfully, he was unwilling to tell them of their new-found freedom.

Satan has no authority over those who belong to the Lord Jesus. The only ground that he can take is ground that is submitted to him. Legal freedom that is acknowledged intellectually lags a long way behind an emancipation that is realised experientially.

Only those who can hold the hand of God and face the past as a totally cleansed environment are secure enough to face the future with lasting confidence. For them Satan the Accuser of the Brethren has, in every sense, been cast down. He whom the Son sets free is free indeed.

Unhealed Wounds

Setting off to run a marathon today with a torn ligament that was incurred yesterday is not likely to prove the most comfortable of endeavours.

Sandra (not her real name) had recently come to faith in Christ. She was conscious of a radical change that had taken place in her life. She was aware that she had entered a whole new world. Everything had taken on a new perspective for her – except, that is, worship. Sandra had even begun to wonder, despite all the clear evidence that accompanied her salvation, if she really had been born again.

Conversation with leaders within her church did not seem to help. It was not until a Christian friend shared with her a picture that she had seen while praying for her that progress began to be made. The friend concerned could see no initial relevance in the picture whatsoever. After all what relationship could a bathroom door with a leather strap hanging behind it have to a new Christian who was finding expressing worship an impossibility? When it was related to Sandra however she broke down in tears. It had startling significance.

It turned out that she had been raised in the home of a father who was both a tyrant and a sadist. From as early in her childhood as she could remember he would beat her with the strap at his slightest whim. In consequence Sandra had great difficulty in relating to God as Father for every time she tried her mind was filled with the threatening spectre of her authoritarian parent. When this was realised, and ministered to, healing took place and her dilemma was over.

This story is just one of a multitude of possible examples that illustrate how past wounds can impede present progress.

I have met, and know personally, sincere and godly Christians who would question the necessity to delve into the pre-conversion experience at all. They quote the text in second Corinthians that says, 'If anyone is in Christ, he is a new Creation; the old has gone, the new has come.'[5] Often their objections to any tending of 'old wounds' have evolved as a reaction to extreme teaching in the area of 'healing of the memories' where, in some cases, untrained and unwise people have attempted to rescue people from an emotional whirlpool before they themselves have learned to swim with success.

A new creation we certainly are; but it needs to be remembered that Paul, in the same letter writes, 'We, who with unveiled faces all reflect the Lord's glory, *are being transformed* into His likeness with ever increasing glory, which comes from the Lord, who is the Spirit.'[6]

The metamorphosis comes about sometimes through painful struggle. The flesh which wars against the spirit bears the genetic imprint of the old nature. Though in failure we are the transgressor and in hurt we are the victim, hurt like failure, must be faced. Part of Sandra's metamorphosis had to do with coming to terms with her feelings towards her biological father. Only then could her feelings towards her Heavenly Father be resolved. Though it is necessary that the past be buried, it must not be buried alive.

It would be a great mistake to assume that any but a small minority of Christians ever have the need to set out on an excursion into the past. There are a few however who do.

What affects most of us in this realm is the importance of keeping short accounts with God and with one another. Wounds untended tend to fester. Lesions become more painful and take longer to heal if they are not quickly cleansed and dressed.

As repentance is the antidote to failure so forgiveness followed by reconciliation are the only antiseptic ointments that can effectively purify an infected wound.

There are those who would argue that their injury has been inflicted not by something that man has done, but by an act of God. 'Where was your God when my son died?' asks the angry mother to the minister she meets. 'In the same place He was when His Son died' the man replies gently, being careful to tread softly amid the woman's sorrow.

Broken dreams and unfulfilled aspirations become to some a blow too difficult to parry. A mark is left. The soreness sobs a perpetual accusation. God again is in the dock. Why has He let it happen?

Suffering makes us either bitter or better. When bitterness ensues, if treatment is not urgently applied, surgery is sometimes necessary. Speaking of it as a growth the writer to the Hebrews says, 'See to it that no one misses the grace of God and that no bitter root grows up to cause trouble and defile many.'[7] Lifting an acorn is one thing, uprooting an oak tree is quite another.

More than one biblical character was guilty of shaking his fist at the heavens. Moses grumbles a short while before thrashing the rock in total frustration. 'Why have you brought this trouble on your servant? What have I done to displease you that you put the burden of all these people on me?'[8] Job, in the furnace of his affliction, says of God, 'All was well with me but He shattered me; He seized me by the neck and crushed me. He has made me His target; His archers surround me.'[9] David, confused and distressed protests, 'Why, O Lord, do you stand far off? Why do you hide yourself in time of trouble?'[10] Habakkuk's complaint was, 'How long, O Lord, must I cry for help, but you do not listen? Or cry out to you, "Violence !" but you do not save?'[11]

Each of these men were hurting and each, through varied and different applications, came to a place of healing that not only closed up the wound but left no scar tissue in its wake.

Three Cleansing Agents

1 *Admitting the fact of anger against God* By pouring out their soul to God these men were at least being honest. Religious cliches were conspicuously absent from their prayers. They were not telling God what they thought He might like to hear. They told Him the truth. All truth sets us free. There is something wonderfully emancipating about honesty.

2 *Taking responsibility for the anger* Hostility towards God is a sin even though self pity tries its best to justify

the pent-up pain. When Moses thrashed the rock in frustration he incurred a severe penalty. He argued that the people were the problem; but God knew better. His temper shrouded a hidden agenda. As God passed sentence He began the summing up by saying, 'Because you did not trust in me enough to honour me . . .'
3 *Repenting of the attitude* Anger, purged of self-pity and repented of, will be forgiven. 'If we confess our sins, He is faithful and just and will forgive us ours sins and *purify us* from all unrighteousness.'[12]

Three Healing Agents

1 *Admitting God's Omniscience* He knows everything. Nothing is hidden from His sight. Perhaps you are reading this today and feel that in some way God has let you down. Broken dreams lie shattered at your feet. Doors have closed. Opportunities that you believed should have been yours have disintegrated like bubbles in your hand as you have reached for them. Healing begins at the place where we admit – God knows what He is doing. Not only the steps of a good man are ordered by the Lord but so too are his 'stops'.

Some years ago I came across this anonymous poem:

Disappointment – His appointment,
Change one letter, then I see
That the thwarting of my purpose
Is God's better choice for me.

His appointment must be blessing,
Though it may come in disguise,
For the end from the beginning
Open to His vision lies.

Disappointment – His appointment
Whose? – The Lord's Who loves me best,
Understands and knows me fully.
He my faith and love would test.

For, like loving, earthly parents,
He rejoices when he knows
That His child accepts, unquestioned,
All that from His wisdom flows.

Disappointment – His appointment,
No good thing will He withhold;
From denials oft we gather
Treasures of His love untold.

Well He knows each broken purpose
Leads to fuller deeper trust;
And the end of all His dealings
Proves our God is wise and just.

2 *Admitting God's Omnipresence* David eventually came to the realisation that the Good Shepherd never ever deserts or leaves his sheep and that not only is He a God 'at hand' but 'close to the brokenhearted and saves those who are crushed in spirit'.[13] When the three Hebrew boys passed through the fiery furnace those who sought to incinerate them were forced to testify that there was with them in the flames one like unto the Son of Man.
3 *Admitting God's Omnipotence* God has only got good plans for us. The Devil has other ideas but of course he always has. Job emerged from hurt to health with the words, 'I know that You can do all things; no plan of Yours can be thwarted.'[14] Habakkuk too came to the same conclusion, 'Though the fig tree does not bud and there are no grapes on the vines, though the olive crop

fails and the fields produce no food, though there are no sheep in the pen and no cattle in the stalls, yet I will rejoice in the Lord, I will be joyful in God my Saviour. The Sovereign Lord is my strength; He makes my feet like the feet of a deer, He enables me to go on the heights.'[15] Not only does God know best but, for those who trust Him, He exerts His power on our behalf. No force is strong enough to thwart His purposes. All His plans succeed. He is Sovereign, not only over the nations, but in all things, global and domestic.

When my wife and I commenced the ministry that we are currently engaged upon it was necessary for us to buy a house in the area we were moving to. We eventually settled upon somewhere that we considered to be ideal in terms of location, size and facility. Then, at the last minute, someone put in an offer considerably higher than ours. It was accepted. Though finding the situation somewhat disappointing we held on to the truth of the text which said, 'Trust in the Lord with all your heart and lean not on your own understanding; in all your ways acknowledge Him, and He will make your paths straight.'[16]

It was several months later that we found out that though we had had a routine survey of the house done there had been problems that lay much deeper. In their haste to block our acquisition of the property the purchasers had rushed into a binding legal contract to buy before clearing the transaction with the mortgage company. By the time the massive structural fault came to light they had been trapped with a responsibility to purchase a property upon which no one was willing to advance funding.

Originally we had concluded that we had been the victims in the situation but the reality was that God had released our feet from what most certainly would have proved to be a severe financial snare. At that time the issue served as a continuing indication that God was in control. The Christian rests in the knowledge that any issue that is big enough to concern them is large enough to concern Him.

Yesterday's Blessing

There is no doubt whatsoever that today God is calling forth a radical people. There can be no place in the current church for attitudes that enshrine and embalm outmoded and obstructive traditions. God always calls his army forward: never backward. Yet those who delight in the title 'radical' can all too easily find themselves teetering on the brink of a dilemma.

One cannot be truly radical and, at the same time, ignore foundations planted in the past. The very word 'radical' comes from the Latin meaning 'root'. The word has gathered an aura of extremism and fanaticism but the scriptural radical desires only to return to fundamentals; to a scriptural foundation and New Testament understanding of the nature and function of the Church.

During the past quarter of a century the church has witnessed the emergence of various groups who felt that they were called to restore the church. They called upon all who would listen to urgently 'jump ship' and leave the denominations to which they belonged and join a purer group. It was clear to them that the vessel was condemned to go under.

The inference was that as God had left denominations it was surely only logical that His true people should also leave and so make the vote unanimous.

In the hurry to run and make their escape, from what was presumed to be an imminently collapsing Babylon, many sought to discard every manifestation of the past. They spoke of leaving buildings to worship only in houses; dismantling the bureaucracy of organisation in order that the church might be purged of politics.

Some of those who have been running the longest are now pausing for breath, confused by the absence of the sounds of crashing masonry. What they considered Babylon has not fallen for it was never Babylon to begin with. They have mistakenly confused denominations with denominationalism. Denominationalism has never been in God's heart; denominations, as we shall see, always have been.

Those leaders within the denominations who did not abandon ship watch somewhat bemused as those that jumped attempt to retrace their steps. They look on as buildings are bought, computers installed and, as far as politics is concerned, create an authoritarian infrastructure far more dominant than most contemporary denominations could ever have imagined possible. Only one thing has changed. Some of these groups, who also tried to 'break the mould', have become marginalised.

The sad fact is that it is not the mould but the church that has been broken and further schismatised: and that by those who proclaim themselves to be the apostles of unity.

When God instituted the family unit – each with parenthood, headship and name – He delighted in their individuality. Those who belonged to the families of the sons of Noah for example saw no need whatsoever to abandon the family headships of Ham, Shem and Japheth and be called only by the name of Noah. Similarly, those many millions of believers who belong to still-flexible wineskins see no need to abandon the headship and framework of authority within the denomination to which they belong.

In Noah's day name-changing was a non-event. Top of the agenda came, 'Am I hearing God?' and, following that, 'Am I in the ark?' It was God's initiative to divide his people Israel into tribes – and, if denomination simply means 'a group with a name', denominational tribes. We read of no account in Scripture of Dan, Naphteli and Asher being called to forsake their tribal families, lose their identities and form a 'one world tribe'. There was no need to. They already were 'one' for God was the architect of a system that would ensure it.

God gave precise instructions where each of the tribes were to camp in relation to one another and this meant that two vital factors would need to be accepted by every individual in Israel. These keys lock the church into God's contemporary purpose and keep denominations from descending into denominationalism.

Recognising Each Other as a Part of the Whole

God did not give the tribes instruction where to camp with reference to their geographical surroundings. That would have been impossible for they were always on the move. The individual tribes were called to camp in relationship to one another, 'Each man under his standard with the banners of his family.'[17] In this act they proclaimed their individuality unashamedly and then acknowledged the tribe next to them as equally a part of Israel as themselves. It is significant that when the land of Canaan was allocated borders overlapped, ensuring that they recognised and appreciated both their own identity and their responsibility and relationship the one with the other.

Left to their own devices there may have been fighting for the central position. There was no way that that could happen now, for the central ground belonged to the Tabernacle, and at the centre of that the Ark of the Covenant, the dwelling place of the special presence of God – the Shekinah Glory.

Denominationalism arises at the point that one tribe declares itself to be the only valid expression of God's purposes – the sole possessors of His Sovereign mandate. I do not hear that voice coming from within the denominations – but I do hear it.

To lock out all that God has done in the past is to throw out the baby with the bath water. Jesus said, 'Therefore every teacher of the law who has been instructed about the kingdom of heaven is like the owner of a house who brings out of his storeroom new treasures as well as old.'[18] The secret lies in knowing what of the old to hold and what to relegate to the past. Those who possess an open mind and an attentive ear will not find it too difficult an exercise.

In an earlier chapter we encountered Elijah in a state of severe melancholic depression. 'I have had enough Lord, take my life,' he says.[19] He had only just stepped down from a confrontation with four hundred and fifty priests of Baal on Mount Carmel. He had met them in a head-on encounter and won. He had been intoxicated with success and today he was suffering the hangover.

For him, like multitudes in our generation, God was locked in yesterday; unable to break out into today. Trapped in time, like a figure in a wax museum, He was remembered only for past exploits. Yet the God who was of help in 'Ages Past' is the very One who longs to make all things new.

We all draw from memories and recount testimonies of times gone by – but these can only be of relevance if the recollection of them injects faith for today. If their only function is to be paraded like fading sepia photographs as evidence for the defence of a more glorious past then the images are better locked away for good. Images too easily become idols; idols too easily become shrines.

3: The Most Powerful Key in the Universe

Recently the television public service department carried a series of special advertisements. It targeted one particular group – elderly people living alone. Callous con men posing as employees of the Gas Board had been visiting houses in pairs and gaining admittance into the homes of the most vulnerable people in society by telling them that there was a suspected fault in their supply. The strategy was simple enough. As one kept the occupant busy downstairs the other went upstairs and rummaged through their possessions searching for valuables and especially for money.

'Refuse to let any stranger over your doorstep without asking for evidence of their authority to be there,' ran the warning. 'Keep the latch chain across your door until you are fully satisfied that their credentials are genuine.' Good advice – not just to the elderly and infirm who are prey to bogus officials – but to everyone who sees the need to keep an enemy at bay.

Before a person becomes a Christian there is often more than a little doubt in their mind that any enemy exists at all. Having come to Christ, and therefore to the knowledge of a personal Saviour, it soon becomes evident through scriptural teaching and through first-hand experience that the believer has an intelligent adversary – the enemy of their soul. At first this can be a frightening revelation. Then, as principles of spiritual warfare are explained, the new Christian is told of their superior position in Christ. Or are they?

Sadly this is too often not the case. Some people fight shy of dealing with the subject. It may be on the grounds that some leaders feel that details are not necessary for the 'ordinary Christian' to know or that the covering of the matter may provoke an unhealthy interest in spiritual forces.

It is certainly true that there are those who have gone overboard on such teaching and who tend to see demons everywhere. They have done discredit to balanced teaching on spiritual warfare. Overkill in some sections of the Christian church has engendered under-exposure elsewhere.

During the desert campaign of World War II, General Montgomery hung a picture of his ultimate rival, Rommel, in his caravan. He found it necessary to keep before him at all times the knowledge that, though he was in a place of comparative security, he had an adversary who was out to destroy all that he and his country stood for. The Scriptures call us to be alert and constantly vigilant of the fact of an enemy that like a lion wanders around seeking whom he may devour.

The most crucial factor in battle is position. If a company of soldiers do not know where they are they are obviously lost. If they know where they are but not where they are in relation to the enemy they are equally at a severe disadvantage. Power to keep the enemy at bay means that not only do I need to know where I am in Christ but also where I am positionally with regard to the enemy.

Closing and locking the door on the adversary calls for a very special security system. In the Scriptures it is called the Key of David. In our generation keys are so small they can easily fit into our wallets or purses. In Bible days keys, especially if they were designed for the gates of a city and could admit or refuse admittance to thousands, were much larger. So large in fact that a man would carry the key on his shoulder in the same posture that a soldier would march with a ceremonial rifle. The Key of David, first mentioned by Isaiah, is powerful not because of its physical size but in relation to the colossal scope of its application. It was first promised to Eliakim the palace administrator under King Hezekiah but later is mentioned as the ultimate key in the universe. As far as Eliakim was concerned it gave admittance to Jerusalem. As far as you and I are concerned it unlocks all the promises of God forbidding entrance to the enemy; destroying his power.

> 'I will place on his shoulder the key to the house of David; what he opens no one can shut, and what he shuts no one can open.'[1]

Later while in exile on the Isle of Patmos the Apostle John receives a message for the church at Philadelphia which includes: 'These are the words of Him who is holy and true, who holds The Key of David. What He opens no one can shut; and what He shuts, no one can open.'[2]

The Key of David

There are over one hundred titles of the Lord Jesus throughout the Scripture. We are not told which, if any, He prefers above the others, but I have often suspected that it is 'Son of David'. He was born into the world in Bethlehem the City of David. When people wanted to worship Him in the highest form imaginable to them they chose to chorus as He crossed their palm-leafed path, 'Hosanna to the Son of David'. When Bartimaeus, frustrated both with his blindness and his inability to reach the Lord, cried out for His attention he did so with what he believed would be the most compelling of introductions, 'Jesus, thou Son of David, have mercy upon me.'

They say that if you want to know how a person requires to be addressed by you, notice the form in which they sign their letters. Jesus signs Himself off in the last verses of the last chapter of the last book in the canon of Scripture in this way: 'I am the Root and Offspring of David, and the Bright Morning Star.'[3]

In the remainder of this chapter we will look at three crucial conflicts and notice the remarkable correlation between them. The fact that you have read thus far tells me something about you. It tells me that you long both for power with God and power over the enemy. As you read these pages carefully you will not only see that you possess the most powerful and potent key in the universe but you will also discover how to use it with faith and confidence. It is a key that unlocks promises and locks out spiritual predators.

A Giant Falls

The story is one of the most well known in the Old Testament: the account of David's encounter with Goliath.[4] Two great armies face one another from opposite sides of a valley, the Israelites at Elah and the Philistines at the significantly named Ephes Dammim – the boundary of blood.

There were two ways to fight this battle. The first option was the one that is part of the most basic scenarios of virtually every theatre of war – an armed struggle in which the strongest defeats the weakest. The advantage with this method is clear in that the conquerors, through their superior skill and might, not only win the battle but reduce the potential threat of further conflict by their massacre of the enemy.

The disadvantage is also obvious. When the victorious armies marched home, though triumphant, their numbers would be greatly depleted and their casualties heavy. It would be little comfort to the women widowed and the children orphaned to hear of a battle won if their own loved ones had been lost.

There was a second option. This was chosen by the nine-foot tall giant Goliath. His suggestion was that, instead of a full scale battle, two champions should face each other. It would be war in miniature but the stakes would be as high as in a total onslaught. Only one person would die; but the army that the defeated champion represented would all become the slaves of the side that won. Goliath picked the fight but Israel were unable to pick a champion. Saul, who was the obvious contender, both because he was head and shoulders taller than any other man in Israel and also because he was king, was unwilling to take up the gauntlet. Young David, goaded by the snarling jibes of the Philistines and unable any longer to see the people of God mocked and ridiculed for their powerlessness, took up the challenge and won.

The Philistines did not immediately run towards the Israelites to offer themselves for servitude – even a giant looked small from the vantage point of a valley's slope. Perhaps their hero was only stunned, not dead. Could it be that this was the end of only one round and that their champion would rise again and, in accordance with his boastful promise, offer presumptuous David's body to the vultures of the air?

As if reading the unarticulated thoughts of his enemies David advanced towards the fallen body of his victim. Horizontal giants hold no dread. With poetic justice David removed from the scabbard Goliath's own sword – the weapon that promised to slay him – and, hacking off his head, he held it high. The Philistines now concluded that Goliath had entered something more than a swoon after all and, as a result, took flight. The enemies of God seldom stick to their own ground rules – especially when it is they who are on the ground.

For a moment we must leave this battle and travel back in time to an earlier one. The earliest battle of all.

An Angel Falls, as does Adam

Lucifer, the Angel of Light and soon to become the Prince of Darkness, was the most beautiful and powerful angel that God had created. Dissatisfied with any position below that of The Trinity itself he instigated a rebellion in heaven and, to use his own words, declared, 'I will make myself like the Most High.'[5]

It was not just a personal vendetta; others were involved in the insurrection. God, always justifiably jealous of His Glory, permits no rivals and Lucifer, together with those angels who followed him, were cast out of heaven.

By the time that Adam and Eve had been located in Eden, Lucifer was already in position. Thwarted, as far as he was concerned temporarily, of his major goal to overthrow God, he settled on a secondary objective – to destroy everything good that God had made.

Adam had been given keys to the universe. He had dominion over everything in creation, from the birds of the air, the animals on the land and the fish in the sea.[6] When the waters of the Red Sea opened before Moses and the sun stood still in accordance to Joshua's command, these great miracles were little more than momentary flashbacks to the kind of authority that Adam had enjoyed prior to his Fall. This is why Jesus, unsullied by sin, was able to speak to water and cause it to be calm, stroll upon it, and even turn it into wine if He so desired. What Keys!

Adam's authority was not his own, in the sense that he had earned it or possessed it as a right. It had been delegated to Him by God. He was a tenant of the Garden and God held the freehold. He swung the keys but it was the Lord who owned the locks. Lucifer saw Adam as a legitimate target for his spite against God. He embarked on the very same ground rules of battle that Goliath would suggest thousands of years later. 'If this is God's prototype man,' concluded Lucifer, 'then this is His Champion.' He recognised too that Adam was more than just a man – he was the head of the human race. As a leader acts on behalf of a nation in the making or the breaking of a treaty so Adam was in a position to put all he represented – the human race – under the same dire curse as himself if he sinned. Destroy this man, concluded Lucifer, and his dominion would also be destroyed.

Satan had wanted Adam but he coveted the keys even more. It is history now. Adam fell and dragged down human nature with him. Losing his rights as landlord he was evicted from Eden and angels were put on guard to ensure than he never again attempted to enter. Adam had lost the keys. Satan it seemed had achieved at least his secondary objective.

Instead of having authority over creation, creation now sought to have dominion over him. Adam and Eve were now at threat from the wild animals and the earth that they had once ruled over. Henceforth the ground would only yield a harvest to them through the sweat of their brow.

There was another parallel with what was to be known later as Goliath's challenge – the vanquished would become the vassals of the victor.

'Everyone who sins', said Jesus thousands of years after the Fall, 'Is the slave of sin.'[7] Because of Adam's transgression Man had become subjugated. Man would try to liberate himself but the gravitational pull of his chains would always serve to drag him down. All would sin. The shackles were too strong.

A Kingdom Falls

A second Adam was needed. Humankind could no longer be trusted for its champion, Adam, had fallen at the first fence. Neither could angels, of all beings, be depended upon, for it was in Lucifer's heart that the seeds of rebellion and insurrection had first taken root. God was to send His only Son.

Panic gripped the Prince of Darkness. From Adam onwards he had watched as mortal men, without exception, capitulated to temptation. It was as if some virile virus had spread throughout the race. Everyone had become a carrier. No one had developed immunity. The symptoms were universal. The plague raged on.

Now the universe hummed with a new development. Angels leant over the balustrades of heaven in anticipation. The spirit world was alive with rumour. A new era was about to be entered. God wasted no time in informing His arch adversary of the day that was now dawning. As soon as Lucifer had sprung the trap God, while the galaxies reverberated with the sound, made His proclamation.

God was fighting no rear guard action. The advent of the Anointed One, The Christ, was no afterthought with Him. It took no one by surprise. The decree had been clear enough. As God had cursed the serpent He had said, 'I will put enmity between you and the woman, and between your offspring and hers; he will crush your head, and you will strike his heel.'[8]

The seed of the woman to which the prophecy referred had now been born – and born of a virgin – for Sin is transmitted through the male line. This was no time now for trees, fruit, and serpents in fancy-dress for this was no ordinary 'Adam'. Satan immediately put it in the heart of Herod to have the baby slaughtered before it could do any damage, yet Bethlehem's baby slipped the net. The Christ Child grew up to face a battery of teenage temptation – never once did He sin. Through his twenties He maintained this miraculous momentum. Entering into ministry He swept everything before Him; lives polluted by sin, He cleaned; bodies ravaged by sickness, He healed; minds tormented by anxiety, He calmed. Like a bulldozer moving through a bomb-site He ploughed on, destroying the work of the Destroyer. It was not dust and rubble that He left in His wake: it was restoration and beauty.

Lucifer longed to nail Him down and eventually did. It was to prove his greatest mistake. As David had drawn from Goliath's scabbard the weapon devised to destroy him, so Christ took the weapon of death and destroyed the Devil with it. As the Messiah had never once allowed sin to cling, now death was powerless to hold Christ within its grip. The plague was stayed. The blood of Jesus had become the antidote – a universal remedy for sin that from that moment was made available to all. As David had held high Goliath's severed head, proclaiming his triumph to ally and adversary alike, so David's Greater Son advertised His mastery over the dominion of darkness for all to see. The Apostle Paul describes the picture: 'And having disarmed the powers and authorities, He made a public spectacle of them, triumphing over them by the cross.'[9]

In the intervening three days between the Cross and the empty tomb Christ descended to the grave and announced to the righteous dead the victory that He had accomplished. The Key that Adam had lost was now regained.

When in a vision John saw Jesus, the Apostle collapsed with fright. Christ comforted him with these words: 'Do not be afraid. I am the First and the Last. I am the Living One; I was dead, and behold I am alive for ever and ever! *And I hold the keys of death and Hades'* (emphasis mine).

A short time later John was also to hear these words: 'Do not weep! See, the Lion of the tribe of Judah, the Root of David, has triumphed.'[10]

The Devil had not only been defeated but he had also lost the keys to his own front door. The first Adam had fallen but the second Adam had regained all that had been lost. As if harmonising all these three great battles together the Apostle Paul writes: 'Consequently, just as the result of one trespass was condemnation for all men, so also the result of one act of righteousness was justification that brings life for all men. For just as through the disobedience of the one man the many were made sinners, so also through the obedience of the one man the many will be made righteous.'[11]

Trusting in Adamic human nature, mankind remains under the curse that came upon him because of disobedience. Trusting in Christ, the believer is removed from the judgement that sin brings; for there is now no condemnation for those who are in Christ Jesus.

We are presented with a choice. We can either associate ourselves with the one who lost the keys, and the authority that went with it – or we can put our trust in the One who regained the keys and the power associated with them.

We began by saying that 'position' is the most important factor in battle and that 'position' means not only where we are in relation to Christ but where we are in relation to the enemy of our souls. Ephesians chapter 1 tells us where we are in relation to Christ: 'We are seated with Him in the heavenly realms.'[12] It also says where Christ is in relation to the enemy: '. . . Seated in the heavenly realms, far above all rule and authority, power and dominion, and every title that can be given, not only in the present age but in the one to come. And God placed all things under His feet and appointed Him to be head over everything for the church, which is His body, the fullness of Him who fills everything in every way.'[13]

Satan is under Christ's feet and, as we are seated in heavenly places with Christ, he is under our feet too. It is vital, if we are to appreciate the power of the Key of David, that we understand precisely why Christ has secured this great and triumphant victory. It was not for His own benefit. He has won the victory FOR THE CHURCH and, if you are a born again believer that means FOR YOU!

Pause for a moment before reading on to consider how this affects your personal life and the life of your family. The Key of David, which is now held by the Son of David for the use of His own sons, holds limitless possibilities. When this Key is turned the lock can never be forced by another, for what God shuts no one can open and what He opens no one can shut. The power of the Key in its application to the individual is reinforced by the words of Jesus to His disciples, 'I tell you the truth, whatever you bind on earth will be bound in heaven and whatever you loose on earth will be loosed in heaven.'[14] This verse is often referred to in the realms of prayer and spiritual warfare, and it does have an application there, though the original context is that of discipline within the local church.

Keys have for generations been symbols of power and authority. In our culture 'coming of age' was at one time symbolised by receiving the 'key of the door'. Today it is no more than a emblem to decorate a greetings card but it is a symbol of a new authority nevertheless. I first consciously linked keys with authority when in the early days of my ministry the church building that our Fellowship worshipped in was burgled. When reviewing security at a meeting of the Church Board it was decided that an inventory be taken of every individual who had access to our premises. Although those who were found to be responsible were in no way connected to the church, it was thought sensible to review our allocation of keys. It was discovered that far more people had access to them than any of us had imagined and that many folk had no use for them at all.

Having completed the inventory, the next step was to recall the keys no longer in use. It should have been the simplest of exercises and in every case but one it was. In one instance however, attempting to retrieve the two inches of base metal was met with the level of resistance that one would expect of the request to amputate an arm or leg. It was clear that, though the key itself was of little value, the authority that it appeared to represent was vitally important to the individual in question. Keys are potent symbols of power.

Sadly there are some within the twentieth-century Church who hold powerful spiritual keys but who seldom, if ever, use them. They would be justifiably indignant were someone to suggest that they should abdicate their positions as sons of God – yet they live their life from day to day exerting no more strength than ordinary mortal men and women. The enemy of their souls does not need to steal their key: only to convince them that the possession of it is enough. They rejoice in their position as children of God, and may even sing with enthusiasm about it, but they never use it as a vantage point to grant them advantage over the Adversary.

God's keys are not made for swinging upon belts. They are designed for turning in locks. Their purpose is two-fold: the emancipation of those who are bound that they might be free, and the security of those who are saved that they might remain safe.

4: Keeping the Enemy at Bay

The previous occupier of the house that we now live in was exceptionally security conscious. He was a Chief Inspector of police and when we moved in it was evident that he had installed almost everything possible to protect the premises. Doors and windows had manual locks linked to an electronic circuit. The major rooms, together with the hall and landing, were scanned by beams that would register immediately the presence of an intruder. As a senior policeman he had probably heard more than once the excuse of a recently robbed householder confessing to an inadequate security system with the words, 'I just never thought it could happen to me.'

The first step to security is the recognition of vulnerability or, to use biblical language, 'If you think that you are standing firm, be careful that you don't fall.'[1]

'Be on guard! Be alert!' Jesus says,[2] and so the installation process commences . . .

A Security System for the Heart

Catherine Marshall relates in one of her books[3] the story of 'The Keeper of the Spring'. He was a forest dweller who lived high above an Austrian village that was situated along the eastern slopes of the Alps. When a much younger man he had been hired by the officials in the village to clear away debris that collected in pools of water up in the mountain crevices that fed the rivers flowing through the town. For years he had maintained his work, walking the hills and removing branches and twigs and anything that threatened to stop the clear, free flow of the water. Most people would be oblivious of his existence and took for granted the scintillating beauty of the streams that cascaded through the village, drawing visitors in abundance as well as the wild life and swans that added to the picturesque grandeur of the beauty spot.

One year the local council felt that it was time that cuts had to be made and all employees deemed to be less than essential to the tourist trade were to be laid off. It was unanimously decided that the Keeper of the Spring should be the first to go.

For a while little change was noticed and holidaymakers continued to flock to the picture book community. As autumn advanced however a marked difference began to take place. The sparkling streams turned yellowish-brown. The smell of stagnant and slimy pools drove off the swans and as they left so fled the hope of future tourist trade. Before long the drinking water became contaminated and disease and sickness took their toll.

It was not long before the old Keeper of the Spring was recalled. It took time but, before many weeks had passed, the village was gradually restored to its former beauty.

His presence had been invisible but, once withdrawn, the results of his absence had been inevitable.

'Above all else, guard your heart,' says the writer of Proverbs, 'For it is the wellspring of life.'[4]

The condition of our hearts reveals not what our declared values are but what our true values are or, as someone has said, 'Character is what we are in the dark'. It is what we are when there is no one around to impress, convince or project an image to. It is what we would be if we could do anything we wished and know that we could get away with it.

Imagine for a moment a driver travelling along a stretch of motorway en route to an appointment for which he is already late. He is aware that the stretch of road that he is on is a notorious speed trap and there is every likelihood that police video cameras and radar devices stretch out across the miles before him. He keeps within the limit.

Re-run the picture in your mind with all the variables unchanged except that this time he now knows that all surveillance equipment has been removed, as have the attending officers. Do his driving habits change? Does he keep within the limit? If not, then in reality nothing has changed. The man was always a reckless driver – even when he ostensibly kept the law.

The Pharisees prided themselves in their strict adherence to even the minutiae of religious observance. They were beyond reproach if measured against the yardstick of legalistic obedience. Glistening religious facades became decidedly dulled when Jesus spoke of another form of spiritual evaluation: 'You have heard that it was said, Do not commit adultery. But I tell you that anyone who looks at a woman lustfully has already committed adultery with her in his heart.'[5]

Few of us would fail to understand the principle that Jesus is teaching. It is however the security measure that the Crime Prevention Officer of the Heart suggests that causes us to catch our breath:

> 'If your right eye causes you to sin then gouge it out and throw it away. It is better for you to lose one part of your body than for your whole body to be thrown into hell.'

It becomes less harsh when one grasps God's perspective on sin. The removal of the conduit through which sin is channelled is not advocated as a punishment for a committed act but as a means of damage limitation. A person trapped in a wrecked car may need to lose a limb that a life might be saved. God alone knows the full ravaging results of sin. His ears have heard the tortuous screams of those in a lost eternity. His body on the cross has borne the punishment of the sins of the world. His heart is wounded at every act of compromise within His Church.

Society may view sin as 'naughty but nice'. God sees it as a wolf at the door, a lion on the prowl, a rattle-snake coiled to spring, a thief about to plunder. The Old Testament typified it by leprosy and the New Testament as cancer. No physical analogy can ever adequately portray it, as the consequences of contracting such physical diseases can only last a lifetime. Sin takes root in time and drags its victim, helpless to struggle free, into eternity. Sin is not to be dabbled in but to be dreaded.

Sometime ago our local television station carried a news item that highlighted a security dilemma that was harassing a local scrap metal dealer. His problem was that at the end of a hard day's work, having travelled throughout the Midlands collecting the source of his income, he would gather it in his yard only to have it stolen while he was asleep. He had tried firmer locks, alarm systems and Alsatians but all to no avail. It seemed that his problem was insurmountable until he hit on what he considered to be his best idea yet. He purchased a lion cub. Throughout the day it was kept in a cage but at night it was left to prowl the scrap yard. The 'Beware of the Dog' sign was taken down and it its place was fixed a daunting notice which read 'Beware of the Lion'.

He never again had a problem with thieves but his difficulties were not at an end. A few months later his predicament was featured again on the local television news. It appeared that one morning he had arrived at his yard to begin his work but was unable to do so. He found it impossible to get the prowling lion back into the cage. The cub had come of age and the very thing that he had taken on board to solve his problems he was now unable to control. The plea was now for someone capable to capture the lion and remove the threat of it from him.

The only purpose sin ever serves is to enslave. It always seeks to dominate. It allows no rivals. None can tame the beast. If resisted it will flee. If embraced it will savage. Sin pays wages and the bottom line is always judgement.

Richard Baxter, the puritan, once wrote, 'Would you have imitated the old world if you had seen the flood that drowned it? Would you have indulged in the sins of Sodom if you had seen the flames which consumed it? Who would have been a Judas who had seen him hanged and burst asunder? Who would have been a hypocrite who had witnessed Ananias and Saphira die?'[6]

God calls us to guard our hearts for another reason too – Blessed are the pure in heart, for they will see God. God calls His people to holiness not for His benefit but for ours. It is very easy to listen to some types of teaching on holiness and be led to the conclusion that God's ultimate purpose is to dragoon everybody into sparkling, orderly, regimented lines – like some cosmic housekeeper unable to countenance clutter.

The message, 'God wants a holy people . . .' is only half the story. The other part is '. . . because those are the ones that He can use, bless, prosper and bring to fulfilment.'

In the twenty-fourth psalm the question is asked, 'Who may ascend the hill of the Lord? Who may stand in His holy place?' and the answer comes, 'He who has clean hands and a pure heart . . . He will receive blessing from the Lord and vindication from God His Saviour.'

Most of us will remember, when as children we were called in from playing to our meal, being asked the question as we approached the table, 'Have you washed your hands?' A negative reply was met with a response that made it clear that cleanliness was a prerequisite for sustenance. At the Lord's table the same question is raised: 'A man ought to examine himself before he eats the bread and drinks the cup . . .'[7]

'Clean hands and pure hearts . . . receive' says the psalmist. The promise is guaranteed under old and new covenants alike and applies equally to answered prayer, guidance, and the reception of all the promises of God.

'No good thing does He withhold from those whose walk is blameless.' 'The prayer of a righteous man is powerful and effective.' 'If you remain in me and my words remain in you, ask whatever you wish, and it shall be given you.'[8]

This is not at all to say that one should desire holiness only for the blessing that it brings. The believer seeks to be holy that they might be like God and for no other reason. However, God has decreed that He will only pour His best blessings into clean vessels.

John Wesley brought both aspects of holiness together when he said, 'Give me one hundred preachers who fear nothing but sin and desire nothing but God – such alone will shake the gates of hell and set up the Kingdom of Heaven upon earth.'

A Security System for the Mind

Before temptation ever reaches the precincts of the heart it must first travel through the corridors of the mind. The mind is the central processing unit of our whole personality. It is so complex that psychologists and neurologists after decades of intense research have only just begun to step on the threshold of the intricacy of its operation. Increased knowledge of its workings only serves to further tantalise us with how much more there is yet to know. What we can be sure of is that we use less than two per cent of our mind's power and that the brain can record no less than 800 memories per second without even getting tired.

From the earliest of our conscious moments we begin to decipher and decode the world into which we are born. We become influenced by our environment and learn to respond to its stimuli. As infants, concepts of behaviour are presented to us as absolutes and we are expected to accept them obediently and without question. As childhood develops we soon become aware of options and choices and thus learn to discriminate between things that differ.

Prior to becoming a Christian our world-view evolves through the perceptions and experiences that we have gathered throughout our life. Then, having come to faith in Christ, we begin to understand our environment not only on the basis of information but also on the evidence of revelation. We begin to walk by faith and not by sight. We discover that formerly the god of this world had blinded our eyes and that now we have been translated from the dominion of darkness into the kingdom of light. The focal point of our affections is gradually moved from the material to the spiritual.

Like the writer to the Hebrews we learn that faith is 'Being sure of what we hope for and certain of what we do not see.' As Moses we persevere; not through trust in human nature or political leadership but through 'Obedience to the Invisible King.'[9]

Given that the root of all sin is rebellion, then one can be sure that as soon as the believer's mind is set on obedience they are considered a legitimate target for the enemy. Knowing this the Christian takes to themselves the adequate defence supplied by God. They are guaranteed complete and total protection if they will wear it. Through God's 'Strategic Defence Initiative' no weapon formed against them can ever prosper and in every temptation He promises to point out the perfect escape route.[10]

In the pages that follow we will begin to infiltrate our Adversary's armoury and systematically scrutinise the weapons that he endeavours to launch against the mind. As we conduct the examination we will need to embark on two other missions. We shall look at the defensive measures and manoeuvres that God has devised to keep us free from their incursion into our life and, most importantly, examine ourselves to see the degree to which we are currently protected.

Discouragement

Some time ago I heard a colleague of mine share this imaginary story with his congregation.

The Devil called all his demons together and laid out a variety of vicious weapons on a table. They were invited to choose and use any that they wished in an assault upon the Christian Church. Each weapon carried both a price tag and a label. One was designated anger and others lust, despair, envy or bitterness. There was a weapon there however that stood out from the rest. The label was turned over. The Devil was asked what this awful instrument was. He replied that this was his very own possession. It was the one that made entry possible for all the others. When the tag was turned the letters spelt out the word – 'Discouragement'.

There is no doubt that Discouragement is a virus that attacks our spiritual immune system and breaks down our resistance to other bacterial infections that threaten our walk with God. The weapon can be wielded by the most unexpected people; even those that you assumed shared your aspirations and dreams and who you considered to be supportive of your spiritual development – fellow Christians. The motivation behind the trigger-finger can be as varied as the application of the weapon itself. It can be fired by the insensitive and the callous, the insecure and those envious of your personal growth with God.

The latter group shoot what has been called 'Volleys from the Valleys'. The picture is of a group of people scaling a rock face. The majority appear incapable of making any real progress but one or two move out from the rest and commence to climb high. Those left behind, feeling belittled by the progress of the few, decide to shoot at them from below. The logic of the assailants is – 'If I can't climb to where you are then I must shoot you down to where I am: no one must be allowed to accelerate away from me.' These arrows of discouragement are always fired from behind – the target is usually the back.

There are some attacks of discouragement that are fired from the front: projected by the hugeness of the task that has to be faced. We are told that the objective can't be reached and, because we have heard it so many times before, we almost begin to believe it. When the people of Israel heard the negative report of ten of the twelve spies they said, 'Our Brothers have made us lose heart.'[11] In consequence a whole generation missed out on the promises of God. Canaan was reserved for those who could believe that God is always as big as His word.

It has also been said that many wounds perpetrated by this weapon are self-inflicted. Failure is sometimes brought about through the setting of unrealistic goals, because of insufficient planning and preparation or an inadequate perception of actual results.

As the weapon of discouragement can come from so many angles God has designed a special shield for it. The Psalmist describes it this way: 'You are a shield around me O Lord, my Glorious One, who lifts up my head.'[12]

Doubt

It is easy to slip into a belief that faith is a force and that doubt is the absence of a force. The truth is that doubt itself is an extremely potent weapon. Doubt is negative power. Doubt does not just stop a person advancing: it sets them in reverse.

Did God Really Say . . .? Doubt was the first weapon that Satan ever used against mankind. He did not say to Eve that God had given her the right to eat from every tree in the garden of Eden for, if he had done, then she would have given an instinctive rebuttal to the lie and gone no further. He chose to ask, 'Did God really say . . .?' He questioned the facts and then followed them by a lie.[13]

Young people heavily pressured by their peers to adopt a secular attitude to living can often feel that scriptural standards are from 'another world'. Of course they are right. The other world is in fact another kingdom. It often seems so much easier to acquiesce in the tantalising option of a conformed comprehension than to embrace the more courageous choice of a transformed mind. The question 'Did God really say . . .?' rears its head in a thousand different ways.

Isn't it too Late now for even God to do Anything . . .? When Martha confronted Jesus on the borders of Bethany there was not a little hurt in her voice as she said, 'Lord, if you had been here my brother would not have died.'[14] Lazarus had been dead and buried for four days and, as far as she was concerned, Jesus had missed both the opportunity for a miracle as well as the funeral. When Christ reached the grave He found a cave covered by a boulder. When He asked for it to be moved He discovered an even bigger barrier present. The barricade to a miracle was present in Martha herself. He recognised its presence as she understandably said, 'But Lord, by this time there is a bad odour, for he has been there four days.'

What Martha was really saying was, 'Lord, if you had come when he was ill we know you could have healed him. Even if you had come when he died, we believe that you could have raised him. It's too late now though – he has gone too far – too far even for God to intervene.'

I meet people all the time who are praying for the salvation of their relatives. It may be their marriage partners or their children. Perhaps you, as you read this book, can remember the time when you longed to see your husband or wife come to Christ, and believed that it could happen, but now you feel it is too late. There was a time when you thought it possible but now you have concluded that they have 'gone too far'. Doubt has overtaken faith and faith has died. It is never too late for God. Nothing is impossible with Him. He who is the Resurrection and the Life can bring back from the grave the rotting corpse of hope – no matter how long doubt has submerged it below ground level. Perhaps your fears are not for another but for yourself? You look back on failure and missed opportunities. Could it be that something that you are struggling with right at this moment, be it habit or temperament, has provoked in you a despair that has killed the dream that you can change. Jesus is still the Resurrection and the Life.

For those who are still in doubt, travel with me back in time to the Early Church. We are at a prayer meeting which is being held in secret. We join it at the point when specific requests are being gathered. The room is usually full but tonight there are empty seats. As the petitions are listed it becomes clear why – those who normally occupy the seats have been dragged off to prison. Mothers and fathers intercede for sons even now under torture. Brothers pray for sisters, and those who do not have close relatives under threat of death feel intensely for those who do. They are all fully aware of the possibility that in a few days perhaps they too will be missing.

Two people are affected by this more than any of the others. Their names are Andronicus and Junias. They are relatives of the man who is responsible for the agonising prayers. His name is Saul of Tarsus, the fanatical Jew who, in his intense hatred of those who call themselves disciples of Jesus, instructs his henchmen to inflict extreme pain upon his victims until they blaspheme the name of the very One they have learned to love. If any man was beyond redemption it was surely Saul. Yet there are those, Andronicus and Junias among them, who as we eavesdrop, we can hear calling upon God for the salvation of the persecutor as well as for enduring grace for the persecuted.

A few weeks later Andronicus and Junias themselves are missing from that prayer meeting and have become items for intercession on the leader's prayer list. As we search for them we find them lying on the filthy floor of a prison cell. Their bodies tense as the footsteps of the guard approaches. A key is turned, a heavy bolt grates backwards and into the small cell is thrown yet another victim. As the heavy door slams shut the two believers pull their new companion towards them. They instantly recognise him and are amazed. It is Paul who once was Saul.

Paul was later to be found at Philippi singing in a

prison. The prison that we now observe was the location where the rehearsal took place. Unimaginable praise is being expressed for the truth that no one is ever so far from God that they are unable to be reached.

Andronicus and Junias appear to be two ordinary and unheralded followers of Jesus yet lesser known names in Scripture became great in God's sight through their determination to deflect the fiery darts of doubt by the tenacious use of the shield of faith. Their names appear only once within the Bible but enough is said of them to portray the events that we have considered. Concluding his letter to the Romans Paul writes, 'Greet Andronicus and Junias, my relatives who have been in prison with me. They are outstanding among the apostles, and they were in Christ before I was.'[15]

The shape of the weapon of doubt is always in the form of a question mark. 'Did God really say . . .?', 'If God is so powerful then why . . .?' 'Does God really love you . . .?'

Heaven has forged a special shield for such onslaughts, 'Let all who take refuge in you be glad; let them ever sing for joy. Spread your protection over them, that those who love your name may rejoice in you. For surely, O Lord, you bless the righteous; you surround them with your favour as with a shield.'[16]

Fear

Three-quarters of the visitors to doctors' surgeries in Great Britain are there because of stress-related symptoms. The origins of the words that we use to describe fear help us to understand the effects that it inflicts upon us as individuals. The word 'worry' comes form the old German word *Wurgen* which means 'to choke or to strangle'. We see an application of this in the parable of the sower where the potential harvest is ruined by the suffocating thorns that sap strength from the earth and destroy its fruitfulness. Jesus identifies the strangulating process in the following way:

> 'What was sown among the thorns is the man who hears the word, but the worries of this life and the deceitfulness of wealth choke it, making it unfruitful.'[17]

In areas of the world where there is an unjust distribution of wealth many people find themselves living far below the poverty line. The powerlessness of existing at a level that forces them to forage for food on a day-to-day basis is a trauma that few of us in the West would find it easy to understand or appreciate. The worries of which Jesus speaks do not come into this category. His focus is on those who, while possessing sufficient to live well on, push themselves to live at a level beyond what they can reasonably afford. For them material possessions are tokens of acceptance and symbols of status. They have been deceived by wealth and deluded by consumerism. The worry of 'not having' in order to survive has been superseded by the worry that they may be perceived by their peers as 'not having.' This is illustrated by the peasant boys in South America who carry with them a stone painted to look like a transistor radio, because they cannot afford to buy one. In the so-called 'developed countries' many take upon themselves unnecessary burdens that, like ballast, weigh them down, cause anxiety and slow their progress. Vast sums of money are spent annually by those whose job it is to convince the public that products are not only available but essential additions to their lives. The conned consumer is the only loser; the advertising industry the only winner. John Harvey-Jones, the former head of ICI is quoted as saying that he earned less than the chairman of one of his smaller advertising agencies.

On one occasion an owl found its way into our church building. It flew round and round the roof area, battering itself against the end walls on each lap of its circuit in a frantic effort to escape. After a while, totally exhausted, the bird lost height until it circled at the level of double doors that had been opened for it. Its self-inflicted pain was the result of a natural instinct that told it that freedom was gained by soaring higher. The truth was that the way out was only to be found by flying lower. 'Flying lower' can prove an emancipating antidote to financially-induced anxiety.

'Anxiety', another synonym for fear, is derived from the German *Angst*. The Latin equivalent refers to a high and narrow passage along the side of a cliff from which there is a fear of falling. Fear of falling down on the job at work, fear of falling down as a good partner or parent are just some of the areas that provoke emotional vertigo. A fear of being catapulted into an unknown future, and especially when that future might involve premature death through terminal illness, is the basis of an anxiety that grips many thousands of people within society every day.

A young minister was called to the bedside of an elderly Christian lady who was dying. This was his first confrontation with death in any form and as he approached the house to visit her he felt anything but prepared for the encounter. He drew by the bedside and, for a while, was unable to elicit any response from the frail form of the weak woman who for many years had been actively and loyally involved in the church of which he was now the pastor. After a while, sensing that there was someone in the room, her eyebrows flickered and she moved her head in the direction of the minister. With something less than sensitivity he commenced the conversation by asking, 'Dear sister, are you sinking?' 'Sinking?' she said, her lips forming a faint smile. 'It's impossible to sink young man. Underneath me are the everlasting arms of God. I could not sink through them any more than I could sink through a rock.'

For her the sting of death had completely been removed and fear with it. She had understood that, for the Child of God, there was no death – only funerals. What we call death was simply God's anaesthetic to take her to Himself.

The shield of faith that douses every fiery dart of fear is painted in the most vivid colours in the accounts of those who have willingly given their lives in the cause of the gospel. The Covenanters of Scotland lived daily with the knowledge that, after the signing of the National Covenant in 1638, commitment to Christ could so easily be followed by commitment to prison and even to death. The first martyr during those days was the Marquis of Argyle who at his execution said, 'I had the honour to set the crown upon the king's head and now he hastens me to a better crown.'

At 4 a.m. on the morning of his execution James Guthrie was asked how he felt. He replied, 'This is the day that the Lord hath made; let us be glad and rejoice in it.' Donald Cargill, approaching the scaffold, is reported to have told the onlookers, 'God knows that I mount this ladder with less fear than I ever mounted a pulpit to preach.'

David said, 'Those who trust in the Lord are like Mount Zion, which cannot be shaken but endures forever. As the mountains surround Jerusalem, so the Lord surrounds His people both now and for evermore.'[18]

When Paul faced shipwreck in the middle of a raging

storm he declared his absolute trust in the ability of God to save everyone on board. After his great confession of faith the sailors took soundings. This done, the conclusion that they came to was that they were in a far worse position than before Paul had prayed. To the Apostle this was an irrelevance. He knew that external factors in no way altered the effective embrace of God's eternal arms.

The three Hebrew boys faced not fiery darts but a fiery furnace. Their faith was inflammable. If God could not be scorched then neither could they; for God was holding them. Later, Daniel was discovered to be inedible – the Grace of God was too tough for the Devil to chew through.

A minister, conducting the dedication service for a new-born baby, has no difficulty holding the infant in his arms. As time goes by the child far outgrows the breadth of that initial embrace. Faith overcomes fear at the point that our mind grasps the truth that no one can outgrow God. The Eternal God will always be a shield to those who take refuge in Him.[19]

Another clue to the adoption of an impregnable defence against fear is found in Paul's writings to the church at Philippi. He writes, 'Do not be anxious about anything, but in everything, by prayer and petition, with thanksgiving, present your requests to God. And the peace of God, which transcends all understanding, will guard your hearts and your minds in Christ Jesus.'[20]

In times of anxiety, prayer begins to work even before we start to speak, for a mind set on such a course has made a statement – 'God is bigger than my fear, He is greater than my need, there is a power outside myself that nothing and no one can overcome.'

Paul speaks of the mind as a city that is surrounded by a great wall. The understanding is that if an enemy is to find entrance he must first pass the gate. However, on the gate there is a guard and the guard's name is Peace. Only one person in Scripture is fully worthy of the title and He is the Prince of Peace Himself – The Lord Jesus.

As Christ is given His rightful place in our life the admission of anxious thoughts are consistently challenged and are recognised either as friends or as foes. If it is discovered that they are emissaries of the enemy then they are resisted and must take flight. This is what Isaiah meant when he said, 'We have a strong city: God makes salvation its walls and ramparts . . . you will keep in perfect peace him whose mind is steadfast, because he trusts in you.'[21]

On a Sunday evening in June 1982 I concluded my gospel message in the same way that I had done in the previous fourteen years of ministry and made a gospel appeal inviting those who were willing to receive Christ as their Saviour to indicate publicly their willingness to do so. I was at that time pastor of the Elim Pentecostal Church in Cheltenham. Those that responded were dealt with by counsellors.

It was not until I was shaking hands with the congregation at the door that I realised that the young boy extending his hand to greet me had been somehow overlooked by the counsellors. Neither he, nor his mother who accompanied him, had been in our church before and I was concerned that he should not feel 'left out' or in any way overlooked. I made an arrangement to visit the family during the week that followed and, the address eventually supplied, I did so.

I arrived shortly before the nine-year-old boy, whose name I discovered was Craig, arrived home from school. Having been made welcome and as I settled into the settee his mother began, 'You probably don't know who I am. My surname is Prime. Does that mean anything to you?'

No one who read national newspapers or watched television in that summer of 1982 could have failed to be unaware of the story of Geoffrey Prime, the man who, whilst working at the GCHQ listening centre at Cheltenham as a top-level linguist, had secretly been in the employ of the KGB and over a number of years had passed on vital information to the Russians. His arrest had only just occurred and the story, which had been described in Parliament as the biggest spy scandal since the Second World War, was on everybody's lips. Rhona shared with me how the trauma had caused her to look to God for the strength to face the ordeal that was only just beginning. Rhona and Craig became committed not only to the Lord but to our local fellowship and a caring church family did all that it could to identify with them and to be supportive. The full story is told in her book *Time of Trial*.[22] On a number of occasions Rhona turned down offers for her story from sensationalist newspapers, choosing rather to tell in her own book, and in her own words, how faith in Christ had brought her through the most testing period of her life.

She was without husband and income and, when he had worked for the Russians he had done so for what he considered idealistic reasons and not for monetary gain. Offers from the media that were in the region of £150,000 could have sounded very attractive to a person in her position at that time. She turned them down. Several months passed before the trial took place and further time dragged by as the family waited to hear the sentence that was eventually pronounced – thirty-eight years. Rhona asked if I would join her in talking to Craig about the implications of the sentencing. By now I had built up a good relationship with him but nevertheless was uncertain as to how I would be able to explain such a thing to a boy who, though intelligent, was still very young. I knew that unless Geoffrey Prime was granted remission he would be eighty years of age before Craig saw him again. As it was I did not speak of time and years; it would have been meaningless to a boy so young – I may as well have spoken about eternity. I talked instead of a heavenly Father whose care was constant and who would never fail, leave or be taken away from him.

As I was about to leave the house I asked Craig about how his hobby was progressing – he collected key-rings from all over the world and I knew that it was the pride of his life. I suggested that he must show me them sometime. His eyes lit up at the request and he asked his mother if he could show me them before I left. Consent granted, I followed him upstairs in the direction of his bedroom. A sight met me that I shall never forget and one that was so moving my eyes were more than moistened as I looked. The scores and scores of key-rings that he had collected were displayed on a huge piece of pegboard that had been fastened to his bedroom wall. It was not the rings but rather the centre-piece that immediately caught my attention. It was the rectangular piece of card around which all the rings were displayed to which my eyes gravitated.

In the centre was Craig' s decision card – the piece of paper that he had signed those months earlier to record his willingness to follow the Lord Jesus. This young boy would not have been able at that time to preach a message on worship but his bedroom wall displayed the most eloquent sermon on the subject that I have ever seen. Though facing a frightening and confusing future, there at the centre of the things that he loved best he had centred his faith in Christ. It was a lesson in Lordship – a commitment to Christ which became the axis around which everything else revolved. He had unknowingly exemplified the truth of the scripture that says, 'There is no fear in love. But perfect love drives out fear . . .'[23]

The love that overcomes fear is not only a love for God but a capacity to be loved by God. It is the consciousness that it is impossible that one who cares for us as much as He does would ever allow anything to come our way that did not work for our ultimate good.

As a small boy it was not the first train journey that I took unaccompanied that caused me the most anxiety but rather the second. On the first occasion my father put me on the train and told me that I would be met by someone when I reached my destination. It never occurred to me for one moment that he was capable of making a mistake or that any arrangements that he had made on my behalf would not be fulfilled to the letter. In consequence I enjoyed the journey immensely.

The second journey was different. This time I remember making my own way to the station, selecting the platform and boarding the train unaccompanied. Having taken my seat I sought confirmation from the person opposite that my choice of train had been correct. Even with such an assurance I was still not fully satisfied. After all, I concluded, as this man was not my father there was a possibility that he could be in error. Perhaps we were both on the wrong train! It was not until I actually reached my destination that my mind was totally free from a sense of unease.

Much anxiety in the believer is brought about by a sense of 'travelling unaccompanied'. We can be aware that Christ has promised never to leave or forsake us but if the theology never takes root within the experience it will float around in the mind, with scores of other restless promises and known truths, and will never become the solid bedrock that trusting faith is made of.

Job knew the evicting quality of 'the love that casts

out fear' a millennium and a half before John ever thought of putting pen to parchment. Torn by trauma he cries out with confidence, 'Even now my witness is in heaven; my advocate is on high. MY INTERCESSOR IS MY FRIEND as my eyes pour out tears to God.'[24]

All of us long to live lives that are free from fear. Most people, given the chance, would exchange almost anything for such a condition. God desires that we abide on a plain higher even than that. He purposes that His people are characterised not only by the absence of anxiety but by the presence of boldness. If such a desire is to become a reality then several anti-fear factors must come into play. These principles comprise our strategic defence against the onslaught of an enemy who longs to see us bowed down and cowering beneath a burden of worry. He knows that unease leads all too often to disease. He is aware that stress-ridden Christians are never candidates for distinguished Kingdom service. God has forged for us a shield of faith. Everything depends on our willingness to wear it.

5: Be Bold, Be Strong

Spiritual boldness is for everyone. It is for you. It is not the prerogative of the super-saint or those with mega-ministries. It is the desire of God for every believer. Those who are bold are those who see the world through God's eyes. Their vision has the capacity to reach beyond present problems and into the precincts of possibilities. Boldness of this calibre refuses to shy away from harsh reality. It is not the spiritual equivalent of 'whistling in the dark'. It is not a fearlessness born of ignorance. It is a courage birthed through street-level faith. Its daring does not derive from 'rushing in where angels fear to tread' but from following in the footsteps of One who has gone on before. Those who are bold will not entertain the possibility that such grounds of faith could ever give way beneath them. Such people will walk on water if Christ has called them forward. They refuse to confuse boldness with impetuosity, for their spiritual stance has evolved out of maturity, not naivety.

In the physical realm weakness and timidity provide an unwelcome accompaniment to advancing years. There need be no such necessary parallel in the economy of God. The young have not purchased the sole franchise on courage, faith or fire. Old Testament patriarchs join arms with the young people of a New Covenant in the same faculty of faith. Youth has its particular advantages but even the old can be bold.

Nor does boldness belong mainly to men. Contemporary Deborahs have emerged because twentieth-century Baraks have backed off. In the past women have played a vital role in the Kingdom of God at those times when there has been a reticence in men to come forward. Today women are realising that God has created them to be far more than understudies who are called to wait in the wings in the hope that they will be 'used' on the stage of God's purposes if the star-role fails to turn up. Rather, living within God's clear order for the family and under scriptural covering and care, they stand alongside their male counterparts in Kingdom activity. Boldness is not owned by either sex or any age group. It is possessed by those who have learned to apply to their lives the following anti-fear factors.

Communion with Jesus

Communion goes far further than petitioning prayer. It is a two-way process. It involves spending quality time in God's presence. Communion is more than the expression of 'wants'. It is a willingness to wait, to enjoy, to listen.

One great President of the United States held an 'Open Court' from time to time. This made it possible for the ordinary people to have an audience with him. More often than not he was called upon to arbitrate between rival parties who had disputes over land rights or the contents of a will. It is said that on one occasion an elderly lady was ushered into his presence. The first thing he noticed as she entered was that she was carrying a wicker shopping basket that was covered with a towel. When he asked her what he could do for her she replied by saying, 'Oh nothing at all,' and removing the small towel to reveal the contents of the basket she continued, 'It's just that I heard that these were your favourite cookies and I thought I might bake you some.'

The head of State was visibly moved. This was the first

person who had ever come before him to give rather than to get. Communion with God is a dialogue of love. It is the place of spiritual reciprocation. A forum for giving as well as receiving. Wherever there is a neurotic impatience to be busy, communion is always relegated to the bottom of the personal agenda. This springs from the mistaken premise that restfulness and activity are mutually exclusive. They are seen as opposite sides of the spectrum when in reality they can, and should, be experienced in parallel.

The writer to the Hebrews speaks of 'running with patience'[1] and creates a picture in our mind so incompatible with our culture that to concentrate on it for any length of time makes the brain hurt.

John Wesley knew the secret. During his ministry he travelled 225,000 miles and preached 40,000 times. In addition he wrote many great works including a home medical handbook that went to some twenty editions. He also organised a free dispensary for the miners. At his death he left behind 129,000 Methodists in Great Britain and the USA. Reflecting upon all his endeavours he once remarked 'Though I am always in haste I am never in a hurry, because I never undertake more than I can go through in calmness of spirit'.

This calmness evolved out of his constant communion with the Lord. He was known to turn down invitations to meet those who were considered to be rich and famous, on the grounds that staying to a late hour might interfere with his ability to rise early in the morning to have communion with the Lord.

When Peter and John proclaimed the message of the death and resurrection of Jesus they were put under pressure by the authorities to desist. Threats of imprisonment and physical pain did not seem to have the slightest effect on them. The Sanhedrin were astounded at their boldness. Luke records, 'When they saw the courage of Peter and John and realised that they were unschooled, ordinary men, they were astonished and took note that these men had BEEN WITH JESUS.'[2]

Prayer

It is vital to recognise that those whose lives characterise boldness have not applied to their lives one anti-fear factor to the exclusion of another. All are present. If our proposition is sound and the theory is consistent with reality it should be possible to look at one example and so expect to discover each facet of the spiritual security system fully engaged.

Those who observed Peter and John had already witnessed their courageous stance under pressure. The next chapter of the book of Acts takes us further behind the scenes. We observe them out of the public gaze of general scrutiny and in the private place of prayer. 'Now Lord,' they say with commanding urgency, 'consider their threats and enable your servants to speak your word with great boldness.'[3]

It is abundantly clear that a lifestyle of constant communion with God preceded this prayer. No one can command the authoritative 'Now Lord' unless they enjoy an intimate relationship with God Himself. Without this prerequisite, prayer is nothing less than a preposterous presumption.

It is essential that those sections of the Christian Church that speak much about authoritative prayer and positive confession do so only in the context of an intercession that emanates out of communion. Unless that is done the use of 'the Name of Jesus' and the calling forth of miraculous acts degenerates into little more than a superstitious symbol, a verbal talisman. At best it is misleading and at worst can irredeemably destroy the faith of those who use the sacred name of God like a fetish and can't understand why the 'wonder' doesn't work.

The miracle fails to spring forth not because the Name of Jesus lacks potency or the promises of God are void of power, but because the words are used in a spiritual vacuum. If, prior to healing the multitudes, the Son of God Himself found it necessary to spend whole nights in prayer with his Father, we may be sure that the same state of intimacy with the Almighty is required of us. The Great Physician is never found emerging from a dressing room primed to perform but rather from the place of prayer prepared to serve.

The world cries out for a Church that can say 'Now Lord' into its hurt and bring healing. It has largely lost confidence in an organisation that according to its perception talks in nuclear megatonnage but performs with all the efficacy of a Bonfire Night sparkler.

There has never been a time when it is more necessary for the Christian Church to come before the Lord in repentance. Some are beginning to discover that performance derives its power from prayer and prayer derives its power from communion.

Filling with the Holy Spirit

Sincere Christians are divided on what constitutes 'Baptism with the Spirit'.[4] What is absolutely certain is that when the Holy Spirit was given to the Church on the Day of Pentecost it did not go unnoticed. The force of it catapulted timid, reticent, defeated disciples, hiding behind locked doors, out into the real world. One hundred and twenty people in an upstairs hired hall, desperately seeking strength, were immediately transformed into a cohesive body of powerful evangelists whose heart was to proclaim Jesus to others. Their numbers were swelled by a factor of twenty-five in as many hours as, on the first day alone, three thousand people were added to the Kingdom of God.

Acts chapter 2 also says that they began to speak in tongues as the Spirit enabled them. However, this phenomenon had not been the focal point or objective of their upper room prayer meeting as they waited upon God week after week.

Those who have experienced for themselves the liberating nature of the gift of speaking in tongues testify to its emancipating ability to release the spirit to worship and the soul to prayer. It takes communion, of which we spoke earlier, into a new dimension. None would denigrate it but, similarly, none should exalt it beyond the parameter of priority that God has set for it.

The one hundred and twenty who patiently prayed were holding on to God for something that He had unequivocally promised would be theirs. They were waiting for power. Jesus had told His disciples, 'Do not leave Jerusalem, but wait for the gift my Father promised, which you have heard me speak about. For John baptised with water, but in a few days you will be baptised with the Holy Spirit . . . You will receive power when the Holy Spirit comes upon you.'[5]

I was baptised with the Holy Spirit some thirty years ago and at that time spoke in tongues. I can remember the day as if it were yesterday. The prayer meeting had been especially convened for those who were seeking a deeper encounter with God. Most of those gathered were in their teens or early twenties. I was on holiday on this occasion and was attending the church of which my grandfather was the minister. He began with this counsel: 'Should anyone be here tonight who supposes that "the

Baptism'' is a spiritual status symbol to be added to the New Birth and water baptism then you will be wasting your time in staying for this meeting. You come to be filled because you are empty, you call for strength because you are weak. Ask not for ''tongues'' but rather call on God for everything that He has got for you – whatever that may be.' He then invited us to begin a time of prayer.

That evening I learned as a young man that Pentecost was not a toy to enjoy; it was a tool to use. Whatever other manifestation there may or may not be, I was sure that if I did not have a deeper desire for holiness and a greater power to witness, then, whatever else I may have experienced, it was not the Baptism with the Holy Spirit. Speaking in tongues is like the light on a car dashboard that reveals that the engine is engaged. It does not however provide information as to whether the vehicle being driven is a Robin Reliant or a Lotus Eclat.

Returning for a moment to Peter and John; the Scripture goes on to say this: 'After they prayed, the place where they were meeting was shaken. And they were all filled with the Holy Spirit and spoke the word of God boldly.'[6]

A Good Conscience

In my previous book *Open Heart, Open Hands* I took time to look at the life of Eli – a man whose responsibility was to hear the voice of God and communicate what he was hearing to the people. Due to an unwillingness to respond to God in total obedience he found it easier not to put himself in the uncomfortable position of being reminded of his sin and, in consequence, failed to commune with the Lord. It is not without significance that the Scriptures record that in those days, 'The word of the Lord was rare.'[7]

When the Christian becomes aware of sin and conscious that it is observed in them by a holy God, if there is not an immediate reflex towards repentance, then emotional and mental energy that would normally be expended in communion is diverted from God and employed instead in self-justification, rationalisation and an attempt to withdraw and to hide.

The writer to the Hebrews encourages his readers to a positive solution: 'Therefore brothers, since we have confidence to enter the most Holy Place by the blood of Jesus . . . let us draw near to God with a sincere heart, in full assurance of faith, having our hearts sprinkled to cleanse us from a guilty conscience.'[8]

When the conscience becomes polluted it is not only our fellowship with God that is spoilt; our relationships with one another are similarly affected. Those whose disposition is characterised by cynicism, criticism and complaint usually are engaged in a subtle attempt to camouflage their own inadequacies. By drawing attention to someone else's they are, they would like to believe, diverting the spotlight from themselves. The things we find most distasteful in others are often the very weaknesses that we are most prone to. When the incriminating finger stabs out its accusation it would sometimes be more accurately on course were it to be rotated by just one hundred and eighty degrees. 'Love', writes Paul to Timothy, 'comes from a pure heart and a good conscience and a sincere faith.'[9]

Nothing negates faith more than a guilty conscience and few things enhance it more than a good one. In the fifty-first Psalm where David pleads before God for cleansing and restitution he implores, 'Create in me a clean heart, O God, and renew a steadfast spirit within me.' Steadfastness, holding on rather than retreating under fire, is the very essence of boldness. That is why the writer of Proverbs penned the truth that 'The wicked man flees though no one pursues, but the righteous are as bold as a lion.'[10]

But what of Peter and John? Does this anti-fear factor have any echo in their experience? We hear it from their own lips. First Peter and then John: 'Do not fear . . . do not be frightened but in your hearts set apart Christ as Lord . . . keeping a clear conscience so that those who speak maliciously against your good behaviour in Christ may be ashamed of their slander.' 'Beloved, if our consciences do not accuse us – if they do not make us feel guilty and condemn us – we have confidence (complete assurance and boldness) before God.'[11]

A Spirit of Brokenness

The compatibility of boldness and brokenness is not immediately apparent. In the realm of the Spirit the connection is essential. Boldness without brokenness breeds arrogance. Boldness in isolation declares, 'I am strong'. Boldness married to brokenness says, 'I am strong in the Lord and in the power of His might.'

We looked earlier in the chapter at the 'Now Lord' confidence of Peter and John. Peter in his time had experienced both aspects of boldness. Three times in his life he is recorded as saying the two most contradictory words ever written – 'No Lord'.[12] We are at liberty to say 'No' to God and we are also free to call Him Lord. What we cannot do by any rules of logic is to use the two words together. When Jesus offered to wash Peter's feet he recoiled boldly with the words 'No Lord'. He was happy to experience God at arms length but Him coming as close as touch was uncomfortable. He wanted a Messiah he could respect and 'look up to', not one who wanted to serve him. Such condescension challenged his ego. If such an act of humility was shown to him by One so great it would surely summon him to respond to others in a similar fashion. There were too many strings attached: too much at stake. If Jesus had acquiesced to Peter's rebuff then the disciple would have been the spectator of nothing more than a dignified religious ritual. As it was he became involved in an intimate encounter with a ministering God. He witnessed omnipotence kneeling; Majesty serving. His bedrock concept of power and dominance suffered a seismic disturbance. Arrogance disintegrated at the feet of love.

John, Peter's companion in a better boldness, is the only one of the Gospel writers to record the encounter. Both learned a lesson that revolutionised their concept of strength and courage.

Peter next says, 'No Lord' in response to the prophecy that Jesus makes with regard to his arrest, death and resurrection. 'This shall never happen to you!' he declares boldly.

Many were able to conceive of a Kingdom in which the Jews were convinced by the irresistible force of the Messiah's teaching, or even of the Romans being overwhelmed by the rollercoaster force of a new political movement. The idea of the Christ suffering, the Messiah dying, was incomprehensible. Peter became at that moment the spokesman for those who always consider victory to be bloodless. Jesus saw in his words far more than a divisive argument; he heard the hiss of the serpent behind the sounds articulated by a human tongue. 'Out of my sight, Satan!', He rebuked. 'You are a stumbling block to me; you do not have in mind the things of God, but the things of men.'[13]

It took Peter a long time to come to terms with human, as opposed to holy, boldness. He was to discover that even the baptism in the Holy Spirit did not give him total immunity to the virile virus of self-will. On the third occasion his voice is softened only slightly as the 'No Lord' becomes 'Surely not, Lord!' However, though marginally mellowed the disobedience remained.

He was staying at the time at the home of Simon the tanner who had a house by the sea. While the midday meal was being prepared he climbed on to the flat roof to spend some time in prayer. In a trance he watched while out of the sky a sheet descended towards him. As it neared he noticed that it was laden with several animals that, according to the Old Testament revelation, were 'not on the menu' as far as a Jew was concerned. When the Lord commanded him to kill and eat, Peter still felt bold enough to say no.

It is clear that the Lord was giving Peter far more than a culinary challenge. The remainder of the narrative records how moments later Peter is invited to take the Gospel to the home of a Gentile, a Roman centurion. Fortunately for everyone, especially the centurion, Peter was obedient and as a result Cornelius was baptised with the Spirit and spoke in tongues, and the message of salvation was set on course to be received by all who would believe, Jew and Gentile alike.

The common denominator that links every bold 'No Lord' response, whether uttered by first or twenty-first century disciples, is the arrogant assumption that the individual believer knows best. Peter implied he was a better judge than Jesus as to what was best for him as a disciple. Prior to the cross he went so far as to suggest that he even knew what was the more perfect path for the Son of God Himself.

Such boldness must be broken. Stop Saul of Tarsus in his tracks, a few minutes before God did, and he would confidently assure you that he was setting out to Damascus on a holy mission with a divine mandate.

Eavesdrop on the prodigal Son as he sets out from his father's home carrying an arrogant air and a bulging wallet and you will hear him tell his loving parent that he knows far better than him how to spend his future. Each of these had to be brought to their knees before they were ever able to find their feet. Peter was to be no exception. 'Even if I have to die with you I will never disown you'[14] he promises with confidence. As Jesus prophesied that before the rooster crowed he would have denied Him not once but three times, the self-assured disciple dismissed the very thought. If Peter had not 'crowed' he would have rendered the ensuing rooster redundant.

When the shrill cries of the bird rent the air Peter's heart was similarly torn. Weeping bitterly, his tear ducts issued forth two great rivers of repentance. He did not know it then but his way down was to prove his way up; his break down would become his break through. Or, to put it in the words of Robert Schuller, 'In Love's service, only broken hearts will do'.

Once we have mastered and applied the Anti-fear factors and we begin to live in boldness we are then in a strong enough position to examine those things within us that threaten the 'principalities and powers'. The secure Christian is challenged, not only to clothe themselves with a system of impregnable defence, but to become aware of those specific issues that agitate the Devil. These factors are not outlined to alarm us but to assure us. Knowing his strategy, and not being ignorant of his devices, elicits a preparedness within us that cannot be evoked in any other way. Those who know what it is to be 'under attack' become stronger by simply knowing the direction from which the barrage is likely to come. Five things particularly stir the enemy.

1 *Numerical Growth*

Those who are part of a growing church or one that is on the brink of numerical increase are a certain target for attack. The Enemy of our souls seldom singles out those who are experiencing spiritual stagnancy. Numerical growth is a threat to him and he will seek every means possible to thwart it. It is not the statistics that scare him but the likely danger that a growing body threatens. He is sometimes more aware of our potential than we are.

In the opening chapter of the book of Exodus the King of Egypt was thrown into a state of near panic. His intelligence officers had just informed him that 'The Israelites were fruitful and multiplied greatly and became exceedingly numerous, so that the land was filled with them.' His solution was to subject them to slavery; to bring them into bondage. It is perhaps significant that many areas of the world that have experienced great revival have later on gone through a time of severe persecution. Though this has not always been the case a clear pattern is apparent. It would appear that a restored church is better fit to face the onslaught.

It is also true to say that those places in today's world where the church lies across an anvil of oppression are the very areas across the globe where the church can be found in its purest form. Fire is not put out with fire. The Exodus story records, 'So they put slave masters over them to oppress them with forced labour . . . but the more they were oppressed the more they multiplied and spread.'[15]

The Enemy always overplays his hand and, in consequence, God causes the wrath of men to praise him. When he attacks a virile church astute leadership will diagnose the problem, identify the cause and direction of the enemy's incursion, call the church together and launch a counter attack. We will look later at the form the counter attack can take.

2 *A Commitment to Holiness*

Few things terrify the Devil more than a pure people. As we have noticed in an earlier chapter, pure people are a people ready to receive, for the psalmist said, 'Who may ascend the hill of the Lord? Who may stand in His holy place? He who has clean hands and a pure heart, who does not lift up his soul to an idol or swear by what is false. He will receive blessing from the Lord . . .'[16] As our Adversary is both a spoiler and a destroyer he is dedicated to the task of seeing that the Church receives as little as possible. Sowing doubt amongst faith, tares amongst wheat and sin amid purity is his very *raison d'être*.

Joshua had been experiencing victory wherever he went. No enemy seemed capable to stand before him. He wisely concluded that if his victories were to continue, and later accelerate, then he must bring the whole of Israel into an entirely new dimension of commitment. He assembled them between two mountains. Half of the nation stood before Mount Ebal and the other half in front of Mount Gerizim. With a copy of the law of Moses, and in the presence of the Ark of the Covenant, he recited the blessings that would accrue to those who would walk in complete obedience, and the curses that would come upon those who chose to disobey the word of the Lord. No one was missing from this memorable event as the whole of Israel made a covenant of Holiness before God. The enemies of God were enraged. They did not call a committee to formulate a carefully worded response; they called for immediate direct action. Hell burned hot with rage. If God's people were to talk about commitment so would they.

The Scriptures take up the narrative: 'When all the Kings west of the Jordan heard about these things – those in the hill country, in the western foothills and along the entire coast of the Great Sea as far as Lebanon (the Kings of the Hittites, Amorites, Canaanites, Perizzites, Hivites and Jebusites) – they came together to make war against Joshua and against Israel.'[17] Their commitment was as unconditional as their targets were unmistakable. Their attack was two-pronged: against Joshua (leadership) and against Israel (the people).

3 *Spiritual Success*

One of the most vulnerable seasons in the experience of the Christian can be in the time following a period of personal victory. It is the moment when the senses are liable to be dulled by complacency and when the ego becomes susceptible to pride. The Spoiler again attempts to plunder blessing.

Abraham stepped out of a special encounter with God only to be confronted with a conflict with Lot's herdsmen. No sooner had young Joseph discovered the purpose of God for his life than he found his brother's hatred stirred against him. Moses descended Sinai to find Aaron encouraging Israel in an orgy of idolatry.

When the Devil finds himself unable to attack the individual in open warfare he will attempt a guerilla action through someone who is 'close'. It concerns him little whether the field of battle is the home or the church; the relationship biological, matrimonial or spiritual; as long as the cutting edge of blessing is blunted – that is all that matters to him. The word of God to the church in Philadelphia was never more relevant: 'Hold on to what you have, so that no one will take your crown.'[18]

When David set his heart to serve the Lord the Scripture says, 'David became more and more powerful because the Lord Almighty was with him . . . when the Philistines heard that David had been anointed king over Israel they went up in full force to search for him, but David heard about it and went down to the stronghold.'[19] The battle is always hotter on the front line than at the perimeter of the field. As David recognised where the attack was coming from, and why, he engaged his personal security system.

The fact that there was a new King in Israel was not what perturbed his enemies. What petrified the Philistines was that the King was anointed. They knew that in Israel such a thing was not merely a secular or civil ceremonial. If David was anointed then the hand of God was on him. If the hand of God was upon him then this leader was unstoppable.

What we see in David is seen in David's Greater Son – The Lord Jesus. He comes to be baptised by John to mark the commencement of His ministry. As he does so the whole Trinity is in attendance. The Son submits. The Father speaks. The Dove descends. No sooner has this taken place than He is led into the wilderness to be tempted by the Devil.

Satan seldom cowers when confronted with Christian talent, scintillating personalities, academic qualifications or leadership skills. However, show him a man or woman who is anointed by God for service and he puts his hosts on red alert.

When God made a covenant with Abraham he commenced by offering him a security system. 'I am your shield' He said, 'And your very great reward.' Abraham listened to the promises that God assured him would be his. In a dedicatory response Abraham offered to God a sacrifice. The moment the offering was presented to the Lord 'The birds of prey came down on the carcasses, but Abraham drove them away.'[20]

Some have offered themselves in sacrificial service to God but have allowed the promised commitment to linger too long on the altar. Today the birds of prey have rationalised the sacrifice until only bones are left. Others, challenged to sacrificial giving, have covenanted to tithe but their purse has been preyed upon by more pressing priorities. God has been small-changed.

5 A Commitment to Build

Determine to grow and the Enemy endeavours to reduce. Aspire to purity and the Adversary attempts to pollute. Seek to sustain success and the Spoiler sets himself to minimise blessing. Aim to serve and the Devil strives to negate the commitment. Venture to build and he resolves to demolish.

When Nehemiah surveyed Jerusalem he discovered that the walls of the city, the testimony of Israel and his own spirit, were all in ruins. 'Come let us rebuild,' he challenged, 'And we will no longer be in disgrace.' This provoked an immediate response from his opponents. It is recorded that they were 'Very much disturbed that someone had come to promote the welfare of the Israelites'. When mockery and ridicule did not achieve the desired result the invective escalated to the point where the enemy was 'angry and greatly incensed'. Unable to undermine the building process they then sought to undermine the authority of the builder. As Nehemiah stirred the people, and the people stirred the mortar, Sanballat and Tobiah stirred the trouble.

Nehemiah's reply was decisive. Refusing to enter into

debate, and having tenaciously kept on building, he set in place his security system. The book that bears his name records, 'When Sanballat, Tobiah, the Arabs, the Ammonites and the men of Ashdod heard that the repairs to Jerusalem's walls had gone ahead and that the gaps were being closed, they were very angry. They plotted together to come and fight against Jerusalem and stir up trouble against it. But we prayed to our God and posted a guard day and night to meet this threat.'[21]

Multitudes of lives lie in ruins, their walls battered. What remains standing gives graphic testimony to the scars of the enemy' s incursion. As in Nehemiah's day, the gates have been burned with fire. Security has been breached, defences are down, peace and purity have been violated; the city has been ravaged.

The ministry of Jesus was to 'bind up' the broken-hearted. The Church only begins to fulfil its own ministry when it too is committed to the restoration of the wounded and the bruised. It takes time to rebuild broken walls; to close the gaps; to rally to the side of the defenceless. The Church has not been called to plaster over cracks, but to reconstruct with permanence.

The Counter Attack

Being aware of the Devil's devices is the most important aspect of Christian vigilance. The essence of security is preparedness.

When the enemy sees the believer advancing into fresh territory it is understandable that he will do all that he can to bring their progress to a halt. Sometimes he succeeds. A new commitment that is met by discouragement and initial disappointment has been known to hinder those who have lacked tenacity. Soldiers, spiritual or secular, are trained to expect resistance and then to overcome it. God gave Israel Canaan but He did not give it to them with vacant possession. They were expected to 'take the land' and where they met resistance, to press on until they made it their own.

When Moses left Egypt he did not leave all his problems behind. Some of the most ferocious attacks came from the very people he was endeavouring to emancipate and even from his own flesh and blood. Aaron was known to antagonise him and Miriam could make him miserable.

In Exodus 17 we read that the people complained that there was not sufficient water. They had been used to putting all their problems down to their Egyptian taskmasters but as they were no longer near enough to blame, Moses came under fire. Leadership often becomes the 'Aunt Sally' to aim at when there is no one else to vent frustration on. In response Moses turns to the Lord with the words, 'What am I to do with these people? They are almost ready to stone me.'[22] When God provided water from a rock the difficulty did not end there. As soon as that dilemma was resolved another one appeared. The people now came under attack themselves – from the Amalekites. Israel realised that they were to fight, not against one another, but against their common foe. The leadership in the form of Moses, Aaron, and Hur could see even further than that. They understood that ultimately their fight was not against flesh and blood but against spiritual wickedness in high places. In consequence they climbed to the highest vantage point that they could find, a nearby hill.

As Moses raised his hands in intercession before God the battle went to Israel; when his hands went down with weakness the battle went to Amalek. Now it was time for his fellow leaders to act. They found a stone for him to sit upon and then supported his hands to make it easier for him to intercede. Earlier, people were looking for stones to attack their leader: now they looked for a stone to support him.

The first act of counter attack is to recognise where the flack is coming from. It may appear to be emanating from those who claim to be fellow-believers. It could appear to be coming from outside. The truth is, whatever the guise, the true battle is with spiritual forces. Those who incite terrorism are as culpable as those who prime the bomb. So too in the realm of the spirit.

When the battle was over and done, and Israel had won, Moses built an altar and called it 'The Lord is my banner'. 'For,' he said, 'hands were lifted up to the throne of the Lord.' This describes the second step in the counter attack.

The banner of a tribe or regiment symbolises the whole body of people. Heraldic emblems sum up the goals and aspirations of the groups that the banner represents. Coats of arms are often accompanied by a motto. God's banner over the believer carries the most comprehensive cover possible. The Song of Solomon simply says, 'His banner over me is love'.[23] When the Church realises, experientially as well as theologically, the fact of God's pure, unbroken, unadulterated covenant love, then trust in that banner alone will put the Enemy to flight.

Another banner also exists to encourage us. David identifies it when he writes, 'For those who fear you, you have raised a banner to be unfurled against the bow. *Selah*.'[24] (*Selah* means 'stop and think' and one should never read through a *selah* without doing so. It is an invitation to meditation.)

It could well be that when the Church rediscovers what it means to fear the Lord its fear of the Devil will be significantly reduced. It is not suggested that we should be frightened of God but rather that we should view Him with respectful, reverential awe.

Much emphasis has been put in recent years, and rightly so, on worship that is exciting and joyous. Church buildings surrounded by graveyards have too often conjured up a perception of death on both sides of its walls. Melancholic worship, as if such a thing could ever exist, has given way to a fresh breath of the Spirit of God. Approachability has been underscored; intimacy with the Infinite has been emphasised; but at what cost? Paul cautioned the Christians in Rome to consider both the kindness and the sternness of God.[25] Not too many stern words are seen embroidered on banners.

Religious attitudes, like pendulums, have a propensity to swing to extremes and polarised positions are rarely right. No one would suggest that the cutting edge of celebration should be dulled but rather that it be whetted by an increased appreciation of the holiness of God.

Fear of the enemy diminishes in direct proportion to a fear of God. An awareness arises that He who is mighty 'over' me will be mighty 'for' me. The fear of the Lord, when raised as a banner before our adversary, causes the foe to cower in that it expresses to him that we do not stand in our own strength but in the power of the Lord of Hosts. It marshals the forces that are for us to stand against the powers that are against us.

Isaiah declared, 'Raise up a banner on a bare hill top, shout to them; beckon to them to enter the gates of the nobles. I have commanded my holy ones; I have summoned my warriors to carry out my wrath – those who rejoice in my triumph . . . The Lord is mustering an army for war.'[26]

An almost standard scenario in a TV Western depicts a beleaguered handful of people surrounded by their enemies, within inches of their last bullet and of their last man, suddenly hearing the sound of approaching hoofs.

Rising to their feet they eventually identify the pennants and banners of their rescuers. Their exultant cry says it all: 'The Cavalry's coming!' The Scripture promises, 'When the enemy comes in like a flood, the Spirit of the Lord shall lift up a standard against him.'[27] Doubt is trust in the Devil's word; its dialect is defeat. Faith stands upon the word of God; its sole vocabulary is victory.

6: Guarding the Lips

When thumbing through my diary I noticed that I had promised a minister friend of mine that I would attend an evangelistic outreach that was being held in his church. When I set out for the meeting I wondered just how many non-Christians would be attending on such a desperate night. Wintry rain fell in freezing diagonal sheets across the path of the car as it ploughed on towards its destination. Entering the hall that had been booked for the occasion I found myself in the presence of around twenty-five other people – all of them Christians.

The visiting evangelist, an American, changed his message in order to bring a challenge to Christians. His theme revolved around the importance of tangible things in our lives and, as he came to the close of what he had to say, he asked the small group to stand. He suggested that it was all too easy to theoretically hand over our possessions to the Lordship of Christ and proposed that we conduct an experiment together. He asked that we close our eyes and conjure up a mental picture of all the major items that belonged to us. If we owned a house, for example, we were requested to visualise it and similarly with our car or cars. That done we were to imagine God's hand reaching out and drawing the object away. His premise was that only if we were able to relinquish things willingly were we truly free from the control of the things that we owned and were therefore able to live under the Lordship of Christ.

As my wife and I lived in a church manse at the time we had no house of our own and so the only thing of any real value that my mind's inventory could summon was my car. I dutifully watched as an imaginary hand drew it away and, as I felt no pangs of panic, construed that I must have, at least in some measure, passed the impromptu test.

The meeting over, and having said farewell to a few folk that were known to me, I made my way out once more into the teeming rain. Approaching the place I had parked my vehicle all that remained was an empty space. The car was gone. It had been stolen! A few days later the police retrieved the car and I discovered a new carefulness in the making of ill-considered vows!

The Power of Words

Jesus spoke of the danger of what He called 'Idle Words'.[1] Idle people are those that, given the opportunity, will not work. Idle words fall into the same category. Scripture says that when we stand before God we will be held responsible for every idle word for 'By our words we will acquitted and by our words we will be condemned'. Given that it is supposed that the average person utters around ten thousand words in an average day one wonders how many of the quarter of a billion words spoken in a lifetime fall into the verbal ranks of the unemployed.

Winston Churchill once accused Ramsay MacDonald of having, more than any other man, the gift of compressing the largest amount of words into the smallest amount of thought.[2] I sometimes wonder if he is not rivalled by not a few Christians for whom perpetual promises of consecration become an almost routine occurrence.

Making appeals at Christian conventions and watching lines of people approach the front for prayer fills me with mixed emotions. The far greater part of me is thrilled that people are responding to the challenge of the word of God. Yet there are times when I observe the procession with just a measure of unease. 'How many of these people,' I sometimes wonder, 'really understand the implications of a commitment to discipleship?'

Speaking in the context of a security system for the lips the Scriptures say

> Guard your steps when you go to the house of God. Go near to listen rather than to offer the sacrifice of fools, who do not know that they do wrong. Do not be quick with your mouth, do not be hasty in your heart to utter anything before God. God is in heaven and you are on earth, so let your words be few. As a dream comes when there are many cares, so the speech of a fool when there are many words. When you make a vow to God do not delay in fulfilling it. He has no pleasure in fools; fulfil your vow. It is better not to make a vow than to make a vow and not fulfil it. Do not let your mouth lead you into sin.[3]

When tempted to temper the force of these Old Testament words we would do well to remember the New Testament experience of Ananias and Sapphira. Lying to God was a capital offence. We expect God to stand by His word and rightly make much of the fact that He is our Father. He expects us to stand by our words on the basis of the same family rule. We are His sons.

James has a good deal to say about the power of words. His anxiety on other occasions was not that they were idle but, on the contrary, when employed wrongly, constituted the most powerful destructive force imaginable.

> The tongue is a small part of the body but it makes great boasts. Consider what a great forest is set on fire by a small spark. The tongue also is a fire, a world of evil among the parts of the body. It corrupts the whole person, sets the whole course of his life on fire, and is itself set on fire by hell. All kinds of animals, birds, reptiles and creatures of the sea are being tamed and have been tamed by man, but no man can tame the tongue. It is a restless evil, full of deadly poison.[4]

Nowhere is this teaching more true than in the context of gossip. The phrase 'idle gossip' is a misnomer. The gossiper may be an idle person but gossip itself is a force with destructive effects that are almost limitless. Few actions cause more damage. It is also wrong to imagine that gossip is only employed in the conveyance of untruths. One definition of a gossip is, 'a person who will never tell a lie if the truth will do as much damage'. Love covers a multitude of sins; vengeful gossip broadcasts them.

Nor is it the case that there is such a thing as harmless gossip. Anyone who has played the children's game 'Chinese whispers' knows how easily a simple sentence is distorted when passed from mouth to mouth. Similarly gossip, progressing from person to person, tends both to gather momentum and increase in gravity.

A businessman whose company manufactured large earth-moving equipment had a press launch for his latest machine. He unveiled is as the mighty 'Model G'. When asked what the 'G' stood for he said, 'Gossip – it moves a lot of dirt and moves it fast'.

The psalmist said, 'Set a guard over my mouth O Lord. Keep watch over the doors of my lips'.[5] Six sensible sentries to put in place are:

1 A refusal to listen: Again, as soon as the story commences the sentry of the mind challenges with the thought 'Friend or Foe?' If what is being said does not pass the test the narrative should be called to a halt. C.H. Spurgeon, when taking up a new pastoral appointment, always refused to hear negative comments about his predecessors. Whenever such stories were commenced he would cut in with, 'As I did not inherit the former minister's cupboard I have no intention to eat of his cold meat'.[6]

2 A willingness to challenge: A minister friend of mine uses a great device to deal with those who come to him with criticisms about another. Drawing from his pocket a diary, his response is something to the effect, 'What you have found it necessary to share with me is most interesting. Doubtless you will want the three of us to deal with this according to the pattern laid out in Matthew chapter 18. Would next Tuesday suit you . . .?'

These first two sentries challenge both the story and the story-teller. What is being subliminally said is, 'Please don't dump your rubbish on my door step.'

3 A refusal to recycle refuse: If the gossip has been relayed in our hearing and we have not had the opportunity to block its entry then, for our part, we are at least able to block its exit. If the aspersion is false, then we would be party to an untruth which, like feathers in the wind, can never be regathered. If it is true, then we have the golden opportunity to ensure that it travels no further. One of the best ways to serve a person is to guard their reputation.

4 Noting who is speaking: The tongue is the thermometer that denotes a person's spiritual temperature. He who talks *to* you of a friend will talk *of* you to a friend. No one can throw mud and keep their own hands clean and, as always, he who carries a tale makes a monkey of themself.

5 Checking the disguise: Security guards are trained to take nothing at face value. Few burglars go to work wearing a striped jersey and carrying a bag marked 'swag' over their shoulder. The worst form of gossip dresses itself up in 'spiritual language'. Examine two statements:

(i) I have heard that Bill and Sue fight like cat and dog. I think their marriage is on the rocks.
(ii) Please pray for Bill and Sue. I hear they fight like cat and dog. Let's trust that the Lord will give them victory.

The rules of war adopted by most countries discriminate between enemy forces found in their territory dressed in uniform and those who are dressed in civilian clothes; punishment for the latter is far more severe. Gossip in any guise will bring an individual under judgement but is doubly reprehensible when dressed up in the camouflage of spiritual concern.

6 Examining the motive: Scandal gains access in direct proportion to our feelings for the person being maligned. If envy, jealousy or any similar negative emotion is present in our spirit then bitter words become transformed all too easily into juicy mortals. The writer of the book of Hebrews speaks of roots of bitterness that spring up and 'defile many'.[7] Though the gossiper has it in their power to cause havoc in the lives of others they also are a great danger to themselves. 'He who guards his lips guards his soul, but he who speaks rashly will come to ruin.'[8]

The Soft Option?

No less than ninety verses in the ever-practical book of Proverbs have to do with the control of the tongue and the sealing of the lips. The most well known is probably the verse which says, 'A gentle answer turns away wrath, but harsh words stirs up anger'.[9]

When James referred to it as the 'unruly member' he was alluding to the fact that the tongue, of all our faculties, is the most difficult to control. Biting back when verbally attacked is perhaps the most instinctive reflex within human nature that there is. Our reactions always reveal more about us than do our actions. Premeditated actions are planned in advance. We have time to think through our responses and operate accordingly: not so with those things we are unable to prepare for.

Reactions reveal all too spontaneously the current condition of our spirit. The grating response of an uncontrolled temperament gives audible testimony to a tongue in gear linked to a mind in neutral. Protective procedures for the lips are incomplete without the safeguards that ensure that our security system is not breached. The secure Christian seeks to ensure that the following factors are part of their day to day walk with God. They are characterised by:

1 A spirit operating in rest: The train had hardly left the station before the guard announced both the presence and the location of the buffet car. In response, a long line of passengers began to pick their way purposefully along the aisle. Steadying themselves against the edges of seats and tables they made their way forward as the carriage lurched and swayed.

Before long the procession was reversed as people returned, their progress hampered further by the juggling of paper plates laden with sandwiches and polystyrene cups filled with unidentified hot liquid refreshment. As the train approached a bend, and a fellow traveller was further jostled as our carriage swayed and rumbled, his hands lost his grip and the contents of his cup lost its anonymity. To his acute embarrassment hot coffee flew in every direction. Those of us who did not get the full force of the shower were as sorry for him as those that did were annoyed. 'This would never have happened,' he said in mitigation of the accident, 'if the lid of my cup had been properly secured.'

Like the hapless traveller, people only really get to know the true content of their lives when their spirit is jostled and their demeanour disturbed. An apparently crystal clear pond will cast up mud and mire as soon as its waters are stirred if such substances have been allowed to settle beneath the surface.

2 An ability to maintain objectivity: No one can 'put you down' without your permission. When a person responds in self-justification, more often than not, it reveals the fact that a raw nerve has been touched. Those who bite back are saying in effect, 'I feel bad about me too, and what you are saying only serves to underscore my lack of self-worth. I am angry with you for affirming my view of myself.' It is the classic reaction of those who feel emotionally insecure. Those who are secure are able to look at criticism a little more objectively. When censured they are able to ask themselves, 'Is what is being said about me true?' If it is they will be the first to want to take steps to rectify the situation.

Spurgeon makes the point: 'Get a friend to tell you your faults, or better still, welcome an enemy who will watch you keenly and sting you savagely. What a blessing such an irritating critic will be to a wise man. What a intolerable nuisance to a fool.'

If what is being said about you is false, and your accuser will not accept your sincere assurances that it is so, then it is clear that it is they who have a spiritual problem that needs ministering to. Those who give the soft answer are the most eminently qualified to help and to counsel.

3 A capacity to operate in love: 1 Corinthians 13 has been called the Apostle Paul's great hymn of love. If it is possible to capture love in literary form then it becomes a willing prisoner in those thirteen verses. Yet this great passage is not only for those who long to learn the essence of love; it has much to say to those who need to know the value of self-control. It is a poem of patience for those who continually live on a short fuse. It is for the emotionally incontinent – those unable to keep their feelings and reactions under control.

> Love is patient, love is kind. It does not envy, it does not boast, it is not proud. It is not rude, it is not self-seeking, it is not easily angered, it keeps no record of wrongs. Love does not delight in evil but rejoices with the truth. It always protects, always trusts, always hopes, always perseveres.[9]

In short: a person who is operating in love is secure enough to receive negative words without feeling themselves to be in any way negated. They are able to understand that a person can reject their point of view without necessarily rejecting them. They have the grace to maintain equilibrium under pressure for they are not thrown off balance by those who do not immediately warm to them. They are able to love because they themselves are loved. They are comfortable with others because they are comfortable with themselves.

4 A refusal to engage in competitiveness: Whole books have been written on the subject of one-upmanship. It has almost become a science. The ability to gain the upper hand, to manage, to manipulate and to control. The desire to dominate breeds a competitive spirit that finds itself unable to parry a blow without fighting back.

To the Christians in Rome Paul writes:

> Bless those that persecute you; bless and do not curse . . . Do not repay anyone evil for evil. Be careful to do what is right in the eyes of everybody. If it is possible, as far as it depends on you, live at peace with everyone. Do not take revenge, my friends, but leave room for God's wrath, for it is written: 'It is mine to avenge; I will repay', says the Lord. On the contrary: 'If your enemy is hungry, feed him; if he is thirsty, give him something to drink. In doing this, you will heap burning coals on his head. Do not be overcome by evil, but overcome evil with good'.[10]

Should this advice be seen to be unpalatable in the society in which we live, it is important to remember the context in which it was first written. These words were penned to people living under the heel of an oppressive foreign power and who lived with their survival constantly under threat. Their possessions, their families and their lives could be taken from them at a moment's notice. The soft answer was never the soft option for these people. Yet they suffered gladly the plundering of their goods, counting it all joy to suffer for the sake of Christ. They did not seek to render evil for evil for they saw themselves as having far more than their oppressors – they had Christ. They had learned that they were 'complete in Him',[11] and that when you are complete you do not have to compete!

Those whose response it is to 'bite back' are aware of their emptiness and smallness of spiritual stature. Those who are able to stand firm under fire are living in fullness and know their true position in God.

An unwillingness on the part of the believer to exact vengeance does not mean that injustice is let off the hook. On the contrary, the argument of the above passage is not whether judgement be applied, but rather, who should apply it. The reason for not taking the law into our hands is in order to 'leave room for God's wrath'.

5 A Willingness to deal with root rather than fruit: Our emphasis on self-control is as relevant as it is biblical yet, if we are to have the most impregnable security system for our lips, there is a stage further yet to go.

Self-control that bites its tongue rather than biting back has not won a complete victory, in the same way that one does not get rid of pride simply by swallowing it. In the Sermon on the Mount Jesus revealed that, even more than our actions, He was concerned with the condition of the heart. Bitter words emanate from a bitter heart. To say the right words while retaining a wrong spirit was dealing with the fruit of the tree rather than the root.

When faced with the Pharisees Jesus put an axe to the root of their hypocrisy when He said, 'You have heard that it was said, "Do not commit adultery." But I tell you that anyone who looks at a woman lustfully has already committed adultery with her in his heart.'[12]

In Jesus we see the perfect expression of obedience, service and love from the heart. He not only spoke the word He *was* the Word. His words were indivisible from His actions as His actions were indivisible from His heart and, of course, they still are.

In Him there was no 'biting of the lip', for all that flowed from His inner being was love. Reviled by violent men, His heart was towards them. Crucified amidst the swirling curses of those He could have obliterated with a single word, His heart, and in consequence His lips, said, 'Father forgive them'.

In life, His control of the tongue emanated from a heart that was totally pure. It was Leonard Ravenhill who said, 'Who but the blessed Jesus could have stood ankle deep in wood shavings, silent and inactive amid oppression, extortion and corrupt religion? Who but Jesus could have kept unbroken silence while eager, strict men, mourning for the delayed arrival of the Son of David, made their loud lamentations at the Wailing Wall?'[13]

In death, the Scripture says, 'He was oppressed and afflicted, yet He did not open His mouth; He was led like a lamb to the slaughter, and as a sheep before her shearers is silent, so He did not open His mouth.'[14]

7: Protection Against a Negative Self-Image

There is nothing wrong about feeling good about yourself; on the contrary, such a disposition is essential if a person is to live in security. God's command that we love our neighbour as we love ourselves[1] is based on the premise that we first love ourselves.

Self-love, in the scriptural sense, is not to be equated with pride. The feigned humility that constantly indulges in self-flagellation and the declaration of how hopeless and unworthy we are does the Devil's job for him. Such an attitude refuses to acknowledge the truth of who we really are. It is the other side of pride; for pride is an unwillingness to acknowledge our true status and, as a result, inflates it.

Self-love does not lie. It allows us to neither diminish nor exalt ourself. It simply tells the truth. It is not complacent but neither is it neurotically fretful. The truth that underpins the self-love that God would have every one of His children experience is gained through knowledge. Discovering who we are in relationship to ourselves, to God, to the Church and to the world, will create around us an indestructible infrastructure – a veritable fortress of faith.

Knowing who I am

In my Relationship with Myself

Everyone has experienced emotional insecurity at some

period in their life. The baby seeking the comfort of food has no vocabulary to articulate its feelings other than the vehicle of its tears yet it is still able to give eloquent expression when communicating: 'I do not feel good about the way I am.'

As we grow and mature our feelings are influenced by other stimuli. We become aware not only of how we see ourselves but also of how other people see us. We may interpret their perceptions accurately or inaccurately but all the time we are building up an internal picture of ourselves. This inner database becomes the reference point from which we choose to react and respond to those around us. Nothing that we think, do or say remains unaffected by it. As everything passes through this central processing unit it is essential that this critical faculty is as secure as it can be.

If a person possesses a poor self-image it will affect the way they respond to others. The most innocent of remarks will be read as a stinging jibe if what is said seems to underscore their own poor view of themselves. Opportunities that are presented will be missed if an individual is convinced that they are far too weak to rise to the challenge.

One day a man passed the shop of a tattooist. Displayed in the window were a host of designs, mottos and emblems that could be chosen from. One particular motif caught his eye. It read, 'Born to Lose'. Annoyed that anyone would be willing to indelibly inscribe such a statement on a person's skin, the passer-by entered the shop to take up the matter with the owner of the establishment.

'Don't blame me', came the immediate response. 'Those words have long been etched on a client's mind before ever they ask me to inscribe it on their body.'

The Bible says, 'As a man thinketh in his heart, so is he.'[2]

Secular self-improvement books have much to say about self-image. Knowing that I would be working on this book, I picked up one of the most popular of these publications at a railway bookshop while waiting for a train. One piece of advice offered was that someone suffering in this way should do all that they could to improve their personal appearance. This, the book suggested, might be accomplished by losing weight, exercising regularly, restyling their hair and restocking their wardrobe. Another chapter gave guidance on how to seek a rise in salary in order to buy the things that 'make life worth living'.

There is no doubt that someone who has been overweight or unfit always feels more vigorous and active once a dietary and exercise regime has been successful. No one would argue either that self-esteem would be difficult to maintain were a person conscious of appearing scruffy or unkempt. There is, however, one undermining common denominator to each of the arguments: each approaches the person as someone who is 'seen' and not as someone who 'is'. The focus is on presentation and packaging and not on wholeness and inner health. To accept these premises one would have to say that those who become disabled, disfigured or redundant could never be the possessors of emotional security and its attendant self-esteem. When those who are disabled or visually handicapped are treated in a patronising and thoughtless way it is often because those who are able-bodied have adopted this former concept of self-image. Through their reactions they convey their own sense of insecurity.

A secure self-image arises out of a sense of inner wholeness and not out of style, status, presentation, power or background. A biblical example illustrates this thoroughly. Take two men: David was a backwoods shepherd boy unknown to anyone but his family and perhaps a few friends. Saul, on the other hand, could not have been more different. Handsome and head and shoulders taller than any other man in Israel he held the most powerful position in the land as King.

Saul became insanely jealous of David and was so threatened by him that on several occasions his passions bordered on the brink of murder. His expression of emotional insecurity meant that any positive remark about David was construed as a negative remark about him. Tormented and intimidated, he did everything that he could to hound David down. He killed all those whom he considered were David's friends, as his paranoic rage drove him to the assumption that anyone who identified with David must therefore be his enemy.

David's resource was not in any outward packaging. Jethro his own father had totally overlooked him as a possibility for leadership when Samuel had come to his home to anoint a King for Israel. As the youngest of his brothers he would never have naturally been considered to be groomed for greatness. David however had a secret, and this factor brings us to our next step towards a healthy self-image. The Scripture records it for us: 'In everything he did he had great success, because the Lord was with him.'[3]

In my Relationship with God

If the believer is to really discover who they are then it is essential that they put the same value upon their life that God puts upon them. Appreciating our worth before God is the only true yardstick that we can measure ourselves by.

There are many analogies in Scripture that seek to describe the various facets of our relationship with God. The Church is described as a Building built around a chief cornerstone which is Christ. It is portrayed as a Bride waiting for its Heavenly Bridegroom. It is depicted as a Body with many parts, all of which are controlled by a Divine Head. On a personal level the individual is illustrated as a soldier under the authority of a Commander; a lamb under the leadership of a Shepherd; a servant in the household of a Master; a subject under the rule of a Sovereign; a son within the family of a Father.

Yet none of these declarations of value, even sonship, match the ultimate affirmation of worth shown in the association between Christ as the Saviour and those who are redeemed. 'Greater love,' says Jesus, 'has no one than this, that one lay down his life for his friends.'[4]

If you had been the only person in the world, Christ would still have died for you. One only has to look at the parable of the lost sheep to see the Great Shepherd – willing to give His life for the sheep – leaving the ninety and nine in the safety of the fold to search for and find the one remaining lamb. That's value!

In my Relationship with my Fellow Believers

One of the commonest characteristics of the emotionally insecure is selfishness. Ironically, wherever there is healthy self-esteem there is also a marked absence of self-centredness. Insecure people are happiest when they are receiving; secure people when they are giving. Whether the currency is money, time, attention or affection the insecure need to be seen to be at the centre of things. No one must rob them of the limelight. Any attempt to do this may be met with a Saul-like ferocity.

The hallmark of the secure is that they love servanthood. They understand the words of Jesus when He said, 'Whoever wants to become great among you must be the servant of all'.[5] Yet when they hear the word 'must' it is not the call of duty but the response of an inner reflex – an instinctive intuition. They are big enough to bend, large enough to love. Secure people have a servant heart.

A man was given an expensive car by a relative. He had parked it in the city centre and on his return to it he saw a small shabbily-dressed boy looking it over.

'How much does a car like that cost, mister?' said the little lad, his face bright with enthusiasm.

'I don't know,' responded the man, 'my brother gave it to me.'

'Your brother! Cor, I wish . . .'

The man anticipated the remainder of the sentence; but was wrong.

'Cor . . . I wish I could be a brother like that,' the young boy said.

One watches the disciples as they squabble over who should sit at the right hand of Christ when it came to Him taking up his throne and compare it with the Lord Jesus donning a towel to wash their feet.

In my Relationship with the World

The Apostle Paul was in no doubt whatsoever as to how he related to those who were yet to hear the message of the Gospel. Four short words said it all – 'I am a debtor.'[6]

He saw himself as a steward of God's grace. A great wealth of knowledge and revelation had been imparted and he saw himself as the executor of an inheritance that was to be shared with the entire population of the earth.

He was obligated to pass it on; to distribute to as many as would receive it.

Recently the rock singer Michael Jackson received $15 million for just three minutes of screen time. It was to advertise a product. The product was Pepsi-Cola. The combined annual budget for the promotion of Pepsi, Coke and Macdonald Hamburgers is no less than a staggering $1,410 million a year. Clearly a great deal of investment is being put into the marketing of junk food and some people are making a fortune out of the promotion. Over the past two thousand years the greatest message of all time has spanned the globe. It has not been spread by individuals making millions but by millions of individuals making nothing and, in some cases, losing a great deal materially in the effort.

Early Christians gave their lives to the jaws of lions whilst others were burned alive. Later, thousands of believers willingly marched into Alexandria, Egypt, during the plague and gave their lives to minister to the dying. Many sold themselves into slavery in the salt mines so that they could minister to fellow believers held in bondage and share the message of salvation with others. They did this in the full knowledge that never again would they see the light of day. Why did they do it? What was their motivation? Why evangelise?

Sin is as cross-cultural as skin. Everybody's got it. It evolved out of man's original disobedience to God in the Garden of Eden and has been, within humankind, a factory that manufactures sins ever since. For centuries Christians have been announcing that the wages of sin is death. That fact is true but, left without further explanation, only tells half the horrific story of sin's consequences. The problem is that most people think of 'death' as being cessation of existence. 'Death is the end?', says the non-Christian. 'Well, that's what I expected anyway. So what?' Spiritual death is not cessation of existence: it is separation from God and all that He is. Hell is a place where everything that God is isn't. In other words it is characterised by an absence of love, light and peace and by the presence of hate, darkness and torment.

Similarly, Christians have been announcing for centuries that through Christ we can have eternal life. Again true – but again only half the story. Everyone has eternal life. Christians have it and so do non-Christians: if by that we mean life that goes on for ever.

There was a time when we were not in existence; in the Garden of Eden with Adam, crossing the Red Sea with Moses, at the feeding of the five thousand, at the battle of Hastings or at the battle of Waterloo. However, now that we have come into existence *there will never be a time when we will cease to be!* When the Bible speaks about eternal life for the Christian the emphasis is on quality not duration. All of us will live forever somewhere.

Every Christian prioritises evangelism over almost everything else because they have experienced at first hand what sin has done to man and know the true nature of its consequences. They believe in Hell as much as Heaven because they, unlike others, refuse to deal in half-truths. They are aware too that the Lord Jesus, through His life, death and resurrection has conquered sin. He has paid its price and, though Himself sinless, has incurred its penalty on our behalf. By taking the full blast of His Father's righteous wrath against sin in His own body on the cross He has removed the possibility of judgement for all those who fully trust in Him for salvation. Through that act He has dealt with the past, promised power for the present and a secure hope for our eternal future. What a message! Who, in their right mind, could keep it to themselves?

An old man, walking along a beach at dawn, watched as a younger man picked up stranded starfish and threw them into the sea lest they should perish in the morning sun. There were hundreds there and he was clearly leaving behind many more than he was able to rescue.

'What good do you think you are doing? How can your effort make any difference?' the old man called across to him.

Looking at a starfish in his hand before tossing it seaward the young man replied, 'It makes a lot of difference to this one.'

What a difference the Gospel has made to us and, knowing what we now know, what Christian, worth their salt and light, would keep the message to themselves?

The Peter Principle

The amnesiac has been chosen more than once as a central character within both novels and films. The plot revolves around the hero or heroine who has forgotten who they are. The whole scenario is devoted to the putting together of small pieces of the jigsaw until the personality of the individual is ultimately clarified.

Peter, having discovered security through brokenness, sets out in just one sentence[7] seven characteristics of the Christian who wishes to know their true identity. He places them before us in order of precedence. We are, he says:

CHOSEN: Scripture teaches that each and every believer has been individually selected by God long before we were born.[8] Even before the world was fashioned God had in mind to draw us to Himself. The elect are not an elite, for they have not been selected on the basis of merit but of grace. However, though the doctrine is as much a mystery as it is a certainty, what Christian could fail to feel secure within such a process?

ROYAL: Peter encourages us to shed our poor self-image. We are children of a King. Within sonship we are heirs of God and joint heirs with Christ. Whatever our secular status may or may not be we are seated with Him in heavenly places. All the privileges of royalty are our possession. No privilege ever exists outside of responsibility and this is why Peter links it to a third factor.

PRIESTHOOD: When John, in exile on Patmos, received his revelatory vision it revolutionised the remainder of his life. As a young man he had had only the most basic of education. This can be easily deduced by comparing his style of writing with that of the Apostle Paul. In the normal course of events he could not have expected to experience anything but a normal, relatively uneventful, family life. His contact with Jesus catapulted him into a world of spiritual power and authority that he could never have even dreamed of being possible. He had witnessed, together with Peter, the empty tomb and in the company of the same man had experienced the endowment of power on the Day of Pentecost. Again, with Peter, he had seen miracles take place before his eyes as he had encouraged people to put their trust in the risen Lord.[9] Following this he had seen the formation of the Early Church and had played a significant part in its beginnings.

Now alone and in exile he would have felt keenly the sense of being jettisoned out of the limelight. Out of sight and perhaps, he even believed, out of mind. He knew, however, that, though separated from others, he was not cut off from God. The opening verses of the book of

Revelation find him 'In the Spirit on the Lord's Day'.

When he encountered Jesus in the vision, though he knew Him well and had been among the closest to Him, he fell at His feet as though dead. The reaction of Jesus to John's weakness was to do two things. The first was to remind John of the identity of His Lord:

> Do not be afraid. I am the First and the Last. I am the Living One; I was dead, and behold I am alive for ever and ever! And I hold the keys of death and Hades.[10]

Later, as John weeps with a sense of weakness, he is reminded too of the powerful position that the Lamb has brought His followers into. They have been made a 'Kingdom of Priests' to serve God.

It may be that there are those reading this book that, like John, feel very much 'out of things'; exiled through ill health, adverse circumstances or advancing years. God's word to you today is that you are as much part of a Royal Priesthood as ever you have been. Others may be aware of their theological 'position' but have difficulty in translating that authority into the tangible world of everyday life. When Moses expressed his lack of natural ability to lead the people out of Egypt God used the very same method with him as he was to use with John one thousand five hundred years later. Reminding Moses of who He was He declares, 'I AM has sent you'.[11] The implication was – because 'I AM' therefore 'YOU CAN'. Having done that God went on to demonstrate His power through Moses in a number of miraculous acts. As always, God looks not for our ability but for our availability.

The New Testament concept of Royal Priesthood is illustrated too by the Old Testament story of Esther.

Vashti having been deposed by King Xerxes, a new queen was sought. When Esther, the adopted daughter of Mordecai, was eventually selected she took up residence at the palace. When the evil Haman sought the annihilation of the Jews he did not know that the queen herself was of that race. The king remained similarly unaware. It was decreed that on the thirteenth day of the twelfth month a mass extermination would take place. As the Jews had no leader to represent them it seemed that their fate was already sealed.

With great urgency Mordecai contacted the queen. Her initial reaction was to express fear for her own life should she intervene. He sent her a second message and it read: 'Who knows but that you have come to a royal position for such a time as this?'[12] Her privileged position meant power and with it responsibility . As a queen she had risen to the ranks of royalty. As a Jewess she had been challenged with the need to intercede. As a part of the royal family she had been charged to speak to the King on behalf of those who did not enjoy the same access.

Since Calvary there has been no need for the mediatorial role of a priest. A sacrifice has been made 'once and for all' for sin and, as a result, 'There is one mediator between God and men, the man Christ Jesus'.[13] The Christian enjoys direct access to God, the priesthood of all believers making redundant and unnecessary all ecclesiastical intermediaries.

The exercise of 'Royal Priesthood' today operates at the point that the Child of God comes before their Father on behalf of those who have not yet discovered Him as Saviour. It takes place when Christian mothers pray for unconverted children; believing children intercede for unsaved parents; colleagues, neighbours and friends approach God on behalf of those they know who have not yet come to faith in Christ. Royal positions imply royal responsibilities.

HOLY: There are those that, if you were to ask them to define what holiness means to them, would commence by presenting a long list of the things that they 'Don't do any more'. Not surprisingly therefore holiness is understood by some to have only a negative connotation. As we have seen in a previous chapter, holiness is God's way of preparing us to receive all that He has in store for us.

Before holiness can be imparted righteousness has to be imputed. God has made us holy. We have been justified not by any works that we have done. The propitiate act of Christ means that the wrath of the Father due to us has been deflected on to the body of Jesus on the cross. Taking the punishment for our sins, Christ has made it possible for us to know the cleansing that has come through the shedding of His blood. He has made us clean. Keeping clean depends on the ongoing work that the Holy Spirit seeks to do in our life as we 'Work out our salvation with fear and trembling'.[13]

NATION: Understanding who we are in the context of a personal relationship with God is important. Taking into consideration the way we relate within the wider family of God is equally essential. We are citizens of heaven who are called to live in relationship with one another under the theocratic government of God.

A PEOPLE BELONGING: If there was one characteristic symptomatic of twentieth-century society it is perhaps summed up by the word 'alienation'. The rise of nationalism throughout the world brings into sharp focus the need for people to 'belong' – to identify with their roots. The attraction of the cults is the 'security' that comes from being part of a closed group in which some are willing to trade-off contact with the many for the sake of a close association with the few. All too late they discover that maximum security is found most often in prisons and so find themselves captives to the bondage that comes from 'belonging at any cost'.

Belonging to God is the essence of emancipation. It is freedom to be ourselves, unbound by habits and other controlling dispositions. It is to do with the liberation that springs from a deep bonding with God, in love. Jesus describes it thus: 'I am the vine and you are the branches. If a man remains in me and I in him, he will bear much fruit; apart from me you can do nothing'.[15] Grafting into the vine was not a painful process for us. It cost Christ Calvary in order that the redemptive transaction could take place. An exchange occurred. We are 'accepted in the Beloved' because Jesus was willing, for our sake, to be 'despised and rejected of men'.[16]

CALLED TO DECLARE: The Gospel has been designed to be preached through doctrine and lived through lives. Valuable merchandising areas in large stores are designated to demonstrators – people who will not only tell us how but show us how.

The first six aspects of status that Peter mentions have to do with 'being' and the final one with 'doing'. Status, and even security, is not an end in itself; it is a springboard that launches credibility into activity. When Paul writes to Titus he speaks of the 'truth that leads to godliness' and later compares that lifestyle with the 'mere talkers' who claim to know God but by their actions deny Him.[17]

Esther may have enjoyed the opulence and prestige of the palace; but that was not the principal reason she was there. Similarly, the Christian has not been seated in heavenly places solely to enjoy the view. The call of the believer to Christ has a clear object in mind. It is no secret why the Church has been grafted into the vine. Jesus spells it out: 'I choose you to go and bear fruit – fruit that will last'.[18]

Knowing I am Growing

Fruit depends upon root. Whether the plant is a vine or a tree, security and stability is dependent on growth that is both above the ground and below it. Visible fruit is dependent upon the invisible growth of the root. The psalmist compares the spiritually productive believer to a 'Tree planted by streams of water, which yields its fruit in season'. Joseph is described in scripture as 'A fruitful vine, near a spring, whose branches run out over the wall'. His growth is perceived in direct proportion to his depth. When Jesus cursed the fig tree for its fruitlessness the disciples later noticed that when it withered it had done so from the root.[19]

Much of my time is spent in travelling on the main arterial roads that link Scotland to England. One such road is lined with tall trees of a similar size and age. A recent storm devastated the forests and felled many of the trees. Travelling the route today, the casualties can be seen lying on the very ground over which they once towered. Those that still remain have not grown taller but they have certainly grown deeper. Houses built on sand are finished far faster than houses built on rock. They may be externally indistinguishable and internally identical yet their security depends not on face but on base. Foundations are ignored at our peril, for nothing conducts a more thorough structural survey than a storm. When individuals become casualties, too often it becomes clear that the root had rotted long before the tree had toppled. When it happens to those who are well known and have grown tall it is because climbing high has been done at the expense of digging deep.

When king Saul fell in battle David took up the lament with the words, 'Your glory, O Israel, lies slain on your heights. How the mighty have fallen'.[20] An examination of Saul's superficial relationship with God in the months preceding his demise leaves no one in any doubt as to the contributing factors to his collapse. None can afford to neglect foundations, for it is especially those that consider themselves to be standing firm that should take the greatest heed lest they fall.[21] There are no corners to be cut when it comes to spiritual depth, for maturity is not just a matter of 'growing up'; it has every bit as much to do with 'growing down'.

A short-cut to a quick profit can prove to be an irresistible temptation to some people. As the woman's eyes glanced again across the faces of the customers in the restaurant she still could hardly believe that it was really him. After all, Picasso, to those who could appreciate his style, was amongst the most popular of painters. 'I'm terrible sorry to interrupt you,' she said with feigned timidity as she sauntered to the side of his table, 'but I wondered if you could sketch me something on this.' She pushed a paper napkin towards him. 'I'm a great admirer of your work and would be happy to pay whatever you like,' she offered as if producing a passport that would usher her into his favour. Though not overjoyed at the woman's intrusion, and concluding it might be easier to acquiesce than argue, the artist drew from his pocket a pen and started to scribble. Having finished he pushed the napkin back towards her adding, 'I hope you like it – that will be ten thousand dollars.' 'Ten thousand dollars,' the woman gasped, 'But you did it in thirty seconds.' 'Madam,' Picasso replied, 'it has taken me forty years to do that.'

We are not told if the transaction was ever brought to a satisfactory conclusion but the story illustrates one thing graphically – experience is expensive.

Most careers commence with exhaustive preparatory training. Unfortunately this does not apply to life itself. Living is learned. Babies tumble before they toddle and garble incoherently before they articulate with clarity. We accept this as the norm and it introduces us to the first of three vital growth factors that always remain constant.

1 Failure is a Better Teacher than Success

Thomas Edison conducted ten thousand experiments before he made the first light bulb. 'These were not failures,' he insisted. 'I just discovered 9,999 different ways that the bulb did not work.'

When Peter clambered, dripping wet, into the boat after the abortive water-walking exercise there is little doubt what was going through the mind of Jesus. I am absolutely sure that He had far more respect for the man with the sopping wet shirt and the sunken ego than He did for the drip-dry disciples with their wry smiles who had never stirred from the security of the boat.

One big American company actually gives awards to its failures – young entrepreneurs who get it wrong the first time but who the company know are the innovative raw material of the future.

Young Christians get it wrong sometimes: unwise in their first venture into witnessing or incoherent in their first attempt at public speaking.

Those of us who are more experienced, who also get it wrong sometimes but who have less excuse, play a major role in the ministry of encouragement when we applaud those who have been willing to 'get out of the boat'. The man who 'hid his talent in the ground because he was afraid' would have been less worried if he had known that there were an 'embrace of encouragers' waiting supportively around him should he fail, falter or fall.

The Skiers Dictum says, 'If you are not falling down you are not learning to ski'. The Bible says, 'The steps of a good man are ordered by the Lord and He delighteth in his way. Though he fall he shall not be utterly cast down, for the Lord upholdeth him with his Hand.'[22]

2 *Pain is a Better Teacher than Pleasure*

Not a few of those who have come to Christ in recent days have done so accompanied by an horrendous and painful past: abused as children, rejected as partners or destroyed by drugs. They are a new creation for which the old has gone and the new has come. Though this is so the 'Enemy of their Souls' would furtively whisper to them in their weaker moments that their past – even their cleansed and sanctified past – discriminates against them when it comes to service. Not so!

Imagine for a moment an alcoholic who approaches the doors of a church building with a desire, not for money to indulge his craving, but for the resource to be genuinely free. The person at the entrance informs him that there are two people who are available to see him and he may choose one of them. The first is the Pastor with a credential in theology and twenty years of ministry behind him. The other is a man who has only been a Christian for a few months but who has been delivered from the clutches of alcoholism and whose life had been radically changed. Who will he choose? The answer is that he will choose the one with whom he can most closely identify, the one who has felt his pain and has learned the language of alienation that accompanies his addiction; the person who has sat where he sits. Ideally he should meet both of them but electing to see the one does not make the other discriminated against. Before the alcoholic has read it he has grasped the truth of 2 Corinthians 1 verse 3 which speaks of 'The God of all comfort, who comforts us in all our troubles, so that we can comfort those in any trouble with the comfort that we ourselves have received from God.'

3 Learning Awakens us to how Little we Really Know

However 'experienced' we might consider ourselves to be the truth is that we are light years away from an understanding of God's full purpose for us. The Apostle Paul wrote, 'I do not consider myself to have "arrived" spiritually, nor do I consider myself already perfect. But I keep going on, grasping even more firmly that purpose for which Christ Jesus grasped me.'[23]

There are few things more nauseating to God than the Christian who poses as someone who has 'seen it all before' and has nothing else to learn. They may well have seen it all before for their spiritual life is probably going round in circles – but that does not deny the fact that there are exciting new locations on the way that their Lord longs to show them.

When the editor of the *Daily Express* was told that there was someone downstairs who could bring moving pictures into the home he called for a security guard with the words, 'For heaven's sake go down to reception and get rid of a lunatic who says he has got a machine for seeing by wireless. Watch him – he may have a razor on him!' The date was 1925 and the man at the foot of the stairs was John Logie Baird, the inventor of television.

We might smile at the thought that such a thing could ever happen; but technical advances in communication between men is as nothing compared to the things that God longs to convey to His Creation. Eternity alone will reveal that those who have claimed to have had the deepest experience of God have merely paddled on the edge of waters to swim in.

Knowing What I Can Become

Our home in Scotland is situated on the edge of what is known locally as the Murieston Trail. The eight miles of woodland that runs alongside a stone-studded stream provides the ideal venue for an early morning walk. Wooden pointers spaced strategically along the way serve to assist ramblers and local people to discover the area to its best advantage.

When first using the route I was happy to travel the suggested circuit but, every time I did, I could not help but be intrigued by one particular point at which several paths intersected. The signpost encouraged the normal course but at the junction there was another track that lay to one side, almost completely hidden by a fallen tree that blocked its access. One day, curiosity having conquered convention, I clambered across the huge natural barricade to see what lay beyond and, in doing so, discovered a part of the countryside more stunning than anything I had seen in the area before.

I have wondered since how many people continue along the normal route of life unaware of landscapes and horizons only marginally beyond them. Occasionally they come to crossroads, but encountering obstacles in their path, imagine them to be insurmountable, at least for them, and in consequence fail to locate whole landscapes of opportunity that otherwise could have come within their vision.

As we have seen in earlier chapters, the past often exacts a heavy ground rent on the territory that we call 'today'. When a person has experienced failure too often they assume that success will always be beyond their grasp. Broad barricades bar their way from ever attempting things again. They conjecture that they are for ever to be manacled to the treadmill of the ordinary and mundane and that fresh fields and new horizons are for other people, not for them. For others the obstacle that impedes their progress and forbids them passage is their sex.

Though there are clear New Testament guidelines for God's order within the family, many of the perimeter fences erected to shut out women from adopting ministry roles within the Church have been set in the solid concrete of culture, rather than theology, and have more to do with prejudice than spiritual perception.

'You are all sons of God through faith in Christ Jesus, for all of you who were baptised into Christ have clothed yourselves with Christ. There is neither Jew nor Greek, slave nor free, male nor female, for you are all one in Christ Jesus.'[24]

The first thing that is noticed after someone has been baptised by total immersion is that they are wet. That they entered the water rich or poor, male or female, with grand social status or unemployed is not immediately apparent, for all who emerge are clothed with the same element – water. Similarly, how we view a person's ministry is not to be based on race, status or sex, but rather, the degree to which they represent the nature and character of Jesus.

It is sometimes argued that the rise of Deborah in the Old Testament was due solely to the ineffectiveness of

Barak, the implication being that womanhood is God's second best. The challenge facing the Church as it prepares to enter the twenty-first century demands the mobilisation of every subject in the Kingdom of God, men and women, rich and poor, young and old, black and white. God is calling forth mighty women to function under the covering of mighty men.

Without doubt the greatest road block to progress is the sense of our own weakness. Nowhere in Scripture are we asked to deny our weaknesses; on the contrary, we are encouraged to acknowledge and confess them. However, having brought our powerlessness into the light, we are inspired to overcome our frailty; to rise and to grow into strength and power. When Paul asks the question, 'Who is equal to such a task?' he answers his own enquiry eight sentences later and says, 'Our competence comes from God. He has made us competent as ministers of a new covenant'.[25] To admit that we can do nothing of ourselves is a positive confession when it is accompanied by the truth that we can do all things through Christ who gives us the strength.[26]

When the Lord told Abram that He was going to change his name, Abram was absolutely delighted. The amendment was long overdue. His friends, family and colleagues did not hear the foreign-sounding syllables as they strike our western ears: they heard the true meaning of the name 'Exalted Father'. Elderly and childless, he would not have been able to count the times when people, meeting him for the first time, had opened a conversation by asking about his offspring and his having to reply repeatedly that he had none. He was to discover that the new name that God was to give was even more onerous, for 'Abraham' would have been understood by those who heard it as 'Father of a multitude'.

However, at the point that Abraham believed that

God was greater than his weakness and stronger than his powerlessness, God performed a miracle through him and, for the first time in a hundred years, he lived up to his name. When Sarah, his wife, had been told of the promise she laughed. God was true to His word and when their son was born he was called Isaac, which means 'laughter'. Henceforth every time his mother was to call her son in for a meal she was to be reminded of the fact that, though God often laughs,[27] when it comes to standing by His own promises He never jokes!

Though we may undermine our own sense of security by belittling our value and worth, God could never be more serious about our potential. To underline His point the Lord invites us to investigate the security system of four of the most defenceless creatures in His creation. His message is: if they can survive and succeed, so can you. Proverbs chapter 30 verses 24–28 fills in the details:

> Four things on earth are small, yet they are extremely wise: ants are creatures of little strength, yet they store up their food in the summer; conies are creatures of little power, yet they make their home in the crags; locusts have no king, yet they advance together in ranks; a lizard can be caught with the hand, yet it is found in kings' palaces.

Store like an Ant

There was never a creature more vulnerable. Its size and strength are so small that it is a miracle that the species ever survived. Not only has it survived but, of all creatures, it is held up to us that we might emulate its example. 'Go to the ant,' we are told, 'consider its ways and be wise! It has no commander, no overseer or ruler, yet it stores its provisions in summer and gathers its food at harvest.'[28]

The harvester ant has developed the habit of collecting seeds in summer and, after removing and discarding the husks, storing them in underground gullies. Aware of its vulnerability, it makes plans in advance to protect itself against those times when winter would bring its weakness into sharper focus. Those who consider themselves to be weak would do well to accumulate resources that will build strength into them. When Solomon encourages us to emulate the ant it may be that he had the words of his father in mind: 'How can a young man keep his way pure? By living according to your word . . . *I have hidden your words in my heart*; do not let me stray from your commands'[29] (my emphasis).

Though the studying of scripture has not lost its appeal among Christians there is evidence that the practice of committing texts to memory has shown some signs of diminishing. The reason for this may have to do with the contemporary teaching methods that do not stress learning by rote. Also, the varied use of modern translations, though important for the purpose of general communication and understanding, has meant that texts are heard and read in different forms, so making recollection more difficult. Though this is so, the studying of Scripture and the memorising of it in any form, is essential to security against the onslaught of the Enemy. The response that Jesus consistently gave to the Tempter when fasting in the wilderness always commenced with 'It is written . . .'

There is great strength too in the storing of those things that we feel that God has said to us in recent days, so that they can be constantly reviewed and meditated upon – recalled so that lessons can be learned and, if necessary, action taken. This may involve the keeping of a diary, a log or a journal of things that have arisen from the preaching and teaching that we have received, from our own devotional communion with God or from personal counsel. Storing them in our summers can prove a tremendous resource when we are able to retrieve them in the winters of our spiritual experience.

A colleague of mine who had undergone imprisonment in a Communist country because of his faith said later on his release that not being allowed the use of a Bible in his cell had meant that he had wished that he committed much more of the Scriptures to memory than he had done.

Yet is not just the winter of the persecution of the Church that we should store for. There is the winter of advancing years when we are not able to be as active as in the summer of our youth, and the winter of trial or ill health at which times those things that we have learned of God can prove to be such a resource.

Climb like the Coney

Those who are serious about strengthening their personal security system never use weakness as an excuse for lack of personal growth. Weakness is no alibi for the crime of spiritual decline. Take three statements, all of which are invalid arguments:

'I am weak . . . so don't expect anything of me.'

'I am weak . . . so I don't expect anything of myself.'

'I am weak . . . so God should understand if I become easy prey to temptation.'

The coney or rock badger as it is sometimes called, is a weak animal and compensates for its natural vulnerability by climbing to higher and safer ground. The psalmist says, 'The crags are a refuge for the coney' and later, 'I call as my heart grows faint; lead me to a rock that is higher than I. For you have been my refuge, a strong tower against the foe. I long to dwell in your tent forever and take refuge in the shelter of your wings.'[30]

There is no one who is so spiritually weak that they cannot increase their security by climbing closer into God. When Nehemiah rebuilt the broken walls of the city he did two things. He made a special point of guarding those breaches in the wall which were the most vulnerable and, secondly, he made every endeavour to build them back to strength as soon as possible. He never once was guilty of underestimating the weakness of his exposed positions or the willingness of the enemy to take advantage of them.

Unite like a Locust

Reinforcing Solomon's profile of the locust, Joel records, 'They do not jostle each other, each moves straight ahead. They plunge through defences without breaking rank'.[31]

A single locust is a sad sight. The smallest child could swat it with their hand – yet it is a most powerful insect. Hundreds of thousands of them flying together can blacken the sky and block out the sun. Descending on a field of ripe corn one swarm can, in moments, wipe out a farmer's entire livelihood. Their unity is their strength. They compensate for their individual weakness by banding together with others who are similarly frail, and so present a frightening fighting force.

Unity has always been essential for security and can be seen in three areas: it is present at the point where a man or woman is resting emotionally secure in the promises of God. The double-minded man, says James, is 'unstable in all that he does'.[32] The Greek word *dipsuchos* literally means 'two-souled' and denotes the doubter who, without the rudder of faith, is blown about by each and every prevailing wind. Domestically, it can be seen in the home that evidences God's order within the family. Where there is clear headship, and parents are living in harmony, their children mature in an environment conducive to spiritual growth. Within church life, a fellowship whose leadership is bonded in commitment to one another create a climate and care within the congregation that is dynamic; an atmosphere in which spiritual and numerical growth is nothing less than inevitable.

As unity is such a source of strength God attaches the greatest importance to it. Should you be in any doubt about that then pause from reading this chapter and write down a catalogue of what you consider is on God's hit-list of the seven most deadly sins. Now compare your list with His. It is to be found in Proverbs 6.16–19. Look at number seven: 'A man who stirs up dissension among his brother.'

Most people are aware of the 'Fruit of the Spirit' listed in Galatians chapter 5. Not all are familiar with the fact that it is preceded by an inventory of the fruits of the flesh. Three of the fifteen flesh-factors, twenty per cent, have to do with the matter of disunity: discord, dissensions and factions.

Roman soldiers used two types of shield. One was circular and particularly useful for hand-to-hand fighting. The other was an oblong shield that had a significant ridge on each of the longer vertical sides. The Romans were known for their discipline in battle. Their adversaries facing them on the field would often rush at them screaming as they advanced. Not so these men. They would stand in long ranks and, at a signal, each would lock his door-shaped shield into the shields of those soldiers standing on either side of him. Instead of facing a line of one hundred infantrymen, their enemies now faced a long unbroken wall of leather, wood and metal.

Their whole was far greater than the sum of their individual parts. Though often out-numbered in battle they were victorious because they were united.

The threat to unity is not always disunity but, instead, individuality. A person may have no desire whatever to hinder fellowship between others but chooses, nevertheless, to remain distant and uncommitted. For them autonomy is a sacred institution and 'doing their own thing' and 'going their own way' are their watchwords. God has created us to 'belong'. Coming together is a beginning. Keeping together is progress. Working together is success. People may withdraw out of pride or even fear but there is security only in community. 'God sets the solitary in families . . . but the rebellious live in a sun-scorched land.'[33]

The words UNITE and UNTIE are composed of the same letters but are opposite in meaning. The difference between them is the position of the 'I'. Selfishness is unity's greatest adversary.

Persevere like a Lizard

The Authorised Version uses the word 'spider' – a creature far more familiar to most of us than the lizard. The faculty that this insect employs to overcome its frailty is tenacity.

The most conscientious housewife, however much she cleans the home, will be unable to forbid entrance to the spider. 'Though it can be caught with the hand,' say the Scriptures, 'it is found in kings' palaces.'

If a spider cannot enter a house through a door it will look for a window and, if that should fail, will find a crack somewhere in order to gain an entrance.

When, through weakness, we fall short of accomplishing our goals, rather than capitulating to failure, those whose hearts are set on reaching their objective will try every avenue until one of them proves successful.

There are few examples of tenaciousness more vividly portrayed in the Bible than the account in Mark chapter 2 of the four men who were determined to get their paralysed friend to Jesus.

THEY WERE NOT INTIMIDATED BY THE SIZE OF THE PROBLEM: They fully believed that Jesus was able to heal their friend and that the Lord provided the only solution to the man's need. Their care and concern for him, combined with their total trust in the power of God, was the motivating factor that spurred them on. Their hearts were like those of the church at Thessalonica to whom Paul wrote, 'We continually remember before our God and Father your work produced by faith, your labour prompted by love, and your endurance inspired by hope in the Lord Jesus Christ.'[34]

THEY WERE NOT PUT OFF BY WHAT OTHER PEOPLE THOUGHT: The King James Version says, 'They sought means to bring him to Jesus' and the 'means' that they found was a mattress. Too many acts of tenacity have lost their grip at the point that the individual has thought more about their personal image than the original objective. The secure stumble when they worry inordinately about what other people may think of their actions. 'Fear of man will prove to be a snare, but whoever trust in the Lord will be kept safe'.[35]

THEY WERE NOT DETERRED BY THE OBSTACLES THEY MET: The first problem that they faced was that, by the time that they reached the venue where Jesus was, the place was already full. Unable to reach the door, they made their way up the external stone staircase outside the house and on to the flat roof. Dispensing with convention and abandoning protocol, they hacked their way through the roof at a point just above where Jesus was standing, and lowered their friend through to Him. Jesus, probably coughing through clouds of dust and peppered with dried mud, not only healed the man but forgave his sins as well. He always rewards tenacity.

Those who seek for Him with all their heart will find Him; those who are hungry for Him are fed; those who are thirsty for righteousness are always satisfied.

The men who hacked through a roof that their friend might be healed would be sure to find a reception from One who would shortly go to a cross that the world might be saved.

He is the epitome of tenacity: 'Jesus . . . for the joy set before Him endured the cross, scorning its shame, and sat down at the right hand of the throne of God' and, encouraging us to a similar endurance, the writer to the Hebrews goes on, 'Consider Him who endured such opposition from sinful men, so that you will not grow weary and lose heart.'[36]

8: Evicting Small-mindedness

Small-mindedness is a destructive force. It seduces us to set low limits on our lives. It causes us to settle for little when God longs to bless us with abundance.

Perhaps the most pernicious effect of the poor self-image, discussed in the previous chapter, is the spirit of poverty that accompanies it. It feeds on the assumption that God's best blessings are reserved for super-saints and spiritual megastars, but not for us.

Some time ago when speaking to a congregation on this subject I asked the following question: 'If I told you that on the way to the service tonight God had spoken to me and said that everyone in the meeting was going to be blessed except one person, how many of you would immediately conclude that you were the "one person" referred to?' Around seventy-five per cent of the people raised their hand!

There are always those who feel that it is presumption to expect God to be generous towards them; to develop ministries and giftings within their life; to extend the borders of their faith. They have concluded, mistakenly, that the essence of humility is to be found in posing as weak and unworthy. They do the Devil's job for him. It is his role to undermine faith and sabotage our potential usefulness; not ours. We play straight into his hands when we hinder and quench the work of the Holy Spirit within our lives. God does not enrich us for our benefit alone. He blesses us that we might be a blessing. He calls us to be tributaries rather than reservoirs. We can only give out that which we have received.

Consider the following verses and, having done so, examine your heart to see how easy it is to distance yourself from their application. Read and re-read them until you can believe that they apply to *your* life. When you have done that surround your current needs within the solid wall of their truth.

> No eye has seen, no ear has heard, no mind has conceived what God has prepared for those that love Him – but God has revealed it to us by His Spirit.[1]
>
> I pray that you, being rooted and established in love, may have power, together with all the saints, to grasp how wide and long and high and deep is the love of Christ, and to know this love that surpasses knowledge – that you may be filled to the measure of all the fullness of God. Now to Him who is able to do immeasurably more than all we ask or imagine, according to His power that is at work within us, to Him be glory in the church . . .[2]

Failure to lock out small-mindedness emanates from a spirit of poverty and a false perception of the sovereignty of God. Those who see the sovereignty of God in terms of passive fatalism will never be filled with the fullness that God desires for them. The posture that articulates 'If God is going to bless me, then He will and I need not endeavour to grow bigger . . .' is totally unbiblical and is no more than pseudo-Christian karma.

The scriptures continually encourage the Christian to strive for perfection, to develop, to covet earnestly the best gifts. Such objectives are not obtained by default. They take place as the individual sets their sights on God's best and stretches every spiritual fibre to attain it.

Three security mechanisms need to be activated to ensure an adequate defence against small-mindedness.

Set Goals – Not Limits

According to the Apostle Paul, a person never reaches their limit until they have attained 'The measure of the fullness of God' and, by any standards, that's full! Those who have stopped growing, whose progress has come to a standstill and whose vision has long since ceased to stretch to new horizons, set their own self-imposed limits. Though an army of excuses be marshalled, the truth is that their argument articulates the suggestion that they know better than God what their ultimate potential is. Each year an oak tree produces enough acorns to populate a good-sized forest. The fact is that only one or two of those seeds ever become a tree – unaccommodating ground and platoons of squirrels see to that.

Every Christian has the potential to live a holy life, win people for Christ, be used in service, be an encourager and exercise spiritual gifts – apart from other areas of achievement. It is not always direct action by the Devil that causes inaction and fruitlessness. All too often growth is stunted by the inhospitable environment of mediocrity and self-imposed limits.

Those who make no profession of faith sometimes put so-called 'believers' to shame when it comes to believing in their innate potential.

In December 1944 Ludvik Hock, a poor Czechoslovakian Jew who had recently joined the army, proposed to his wife. He promised her that he would 'Win a Military Cross, make his fortune and make her happy until the end of his days'.[3] By the end of the war he had won the coveted medal and is today one of the richest men in the world. He is known better by the name he later gave himself – Robert Maxwell. He set no limit – only goals.

In 1844 Michael Marks set up a market stall in Leeds with the help of his friend Tom Spencer. Their goal was the production of goods that would provide high quality and value for money. Today Marks and Spencer is a multi-million pound industry that sets the highest standards in merchandising and employs over 30,000 people.[4] No limits – only goals.

What place have such secular stories in a chapter like this?

Although every Christian may not be destined for financial prosperity and commercial success an underlying factor demands our attention. The following words of Jesus need to be heard: 'The people of this world are more shrewd in dealing with their own kind than are the people of light'.[5]

Commercial success does not happen by chance. It is the result of investment, total commitment, strenuous effort and sometimes sacrifice. When the goal is money no cost is too great.

Why did Jesus draw such a parallel?

He knew that a time would come when there would be those who would be willing to spend £4 million to buy ten minutes on television to advertise a soap powder[6] whilst, at the same time, there would be Christians who would be unwilling to spend ten minutes a day to seek the face of God.

Christ constantly calls His people to cast aside mediocrity, and the small-mindedness that accompanies it, to achieve His highest and His best for themselves, their families and their church.

Too few Christians set goals. In some quarters it is even considered unspiritual to do so. In others it is convenient not to for, if an archer does not have a target, he cannot ever be accused of having missed the mark. Goals are essential to progress. The eminent psychiatrist Carl Jung has said:

> The vast neurotic misery of the world could be termed a neurosis of emptiness. Men cut themselves off from the root of their being, from God, and then life turns empty, inane, meaningless, without purpose. So when God goes goal goes. When goal goes, meaning goes. When meaning goes, value goes and life turns dead on our hands.

Where goals do exist they are sometimes little more than a desire for general personal blessing. Imagine for a moment a man standing in a long queue at a railway station. When he eventually arrives at the reservation window and is asked what he wants he says, 'A ticket please'. The obvious retort by the clerk will be 'A ticket to where?' A general prayer says 'Bless me please'. God replies, 'Bless you how?'

In Mark chapter 10 James and John approached Jesus with the words, 'Teacher, we want you to do for us whatever we ask'.[7] 'What do you want me to do?' Jesus replied – encouraging them to be more specific. When they told Him He found it impossible to accede to their request. In this case their precision precluded a positive reply. They were seeking status rather than servanthood. Their goal and God's goals for them were at opposite ends of the Kingdom spectrum.

A few verses later, in the same chapter, we find blind Bartimaeus pushing through the crowd to get closer to the Lord. Jesus asked him the very question He had previously asked His disciples – 'What do you want me to do for you?' When Bartimaeus asked for his sight the

Master replied, 'Go, your faith has healed you'.

Defining our request does not mean that we are more likely to get the answer we are looking for. Neither does God call us to be specific out of a sense of bureaucratic orderliness or a need for a precise form of words. Delineating our request sets a demarcation line around our faith. It expresses that we know what we are aiming for from God and have faith to believe that God is able to do it. Had Bartimaeus merely been asking for a blessing Jesus could have answered that by simply giving him a generous contribution to his begging bowl.

Remember – Good is the Enemy of the Best

Mediocrity is inseparably married to complacency. When something has been done well it is all too easy to see that object as the final product: a destination rather than a milestone. Few things hinder progress more than the false premise that because something is good it cannot be improved upon.

Probably no one this century changed the industrial landscape of the world more than Henry Ford. His famous Model T motor car caused nothing short of a social revolution. It is said that, on hearing that one of his engineers had developed cars which were variations on his theme, in order to give more choice to the consumer, he broke into the workshop and smashed the threatening vehicles to pieces. That which was good had become the enemy of that which could be done better.

It has been said that to the fearful change is threatening because they worry that things may get worse. To the hopeful change is encouraging because they feel that things may get better. If change is intimidating to those who are called upon to adjust to it, how much more traumatic it can prove to be to those who are called upon to initiate it.

Machiavelli spoke of the champion's plight in *The Prince*:

> It ought to be remembered that there is nothing more difficult to take in hand, more perilous to conduct, or more uncertain in its success, that to take the lead in the introduction of a new order of things. Because the innovator has for enemies all those who have done well under the old conditions, and lukewarm defenders among those who may do well under the new.

Tom Peters, co-author of the classic management book *In Search Of Excellence*, says in his latest work, 'Today's successful business leaders will be those who are most flexible of mind . . . Success will come to those who love constant change, not those who attempt to eliminate it . . . Failure today is a failure to change.'[8]

All progress demands change. A person travelling to a country they have never visited before will accept that they will see and experience things they have never seen before. They will take for granted that they will be travelling new roads, not the old familiar tracks. Those who resist helpful progressive change are the guardians of mediocrity. Their experience is more likely to be circular than linear, travelling round rather than pressing on.

As a boy I well remember the old hymn 'Higher Ground' being sung at our church. In it the authors call for freshness, growth, change of perspective, new and deeper experiences.

> I'm pressing on the upward way,
> New heights I'm gaining every day;
> Still praying as I onward bound,
> 'Lord plant my feet on higher ground.'

My heart has no desire to stay
Where doubts arise, and fears dismay;
Though some may dwell where these abound,
My constant aim is higher ground.[9]

At Horeb the Lord spoke to Israel and said, 'You have circled this mountain long enough. Break camp and advance . . . see, I have given you this land. Go in and take possession . . .'[10]

God made reference not only to a need to move on but to a crucial time factor. Yesterday's success, if dwelt on to inordinate lengths, may threaten to jeopardise tomorrow's victory.

It was James Russell Lowell who wrote:

Life is a leaf of paper white
Whereon each one of us may write
His word or two, and then comes night.

Or in the words of Disraeli, 'Life is too short to be little'.

Changing Emotional Polarity

When a person comes to Christ He transforms them into a new creation without destroying their personality. If they were extroverts before they remain extroverts on the other side of conversion – unless of course that trait was an emotional mask covering up an insecurity that required reparation and healing. Individuality is not erased at the point a person commits their life to the Lord. Prior to his conversion the most noticeable characteristics of the Apostle Paul were his energy and his zeal. Speaking about these attributes he said:

I persecuted the followers of this Way to their death, arresting both men and women and throwing them into

> prison, as also the high priest and all the council can testify. I even obtained letters from them to their brothers in Damascus, and went there to bring these people as prisoners to Jerusalem to be punished.[11]

When he became a Christian his zeal was, once again, a hallmark and feature of his demeanour. The difference was that it had been redirected. Now it was said of him, 'The man who formerly persecuted us is now preaching the faith he was trying to destroy'.[12]

He remained enthusiastic about what we might call door-to-door work. Formerly it consisted of destroying the Church by 'going from house to house to drag men and women off to prison'. Now it was characterised by building the Church through 'teaching publicly and from house to house'.[13]

A parallel can be seen in the floodwater that bursts the bank of a river, threatening the livelihood of farmers and the economy of the area which, when controlled and harnessed by dams, serves to irrigate the very pasture it once put at peril.

Allowing our emotions to be re-polarised, to be transformed from that which is negative and destructive to that which is positive and attractive, is a major step on the road to spiritual maturity.

Anger

Anger need not be negative. As an emotion it is amoral. Like any weapon, it only becomes right or wrong depending on the object on which it is targeted. The Scriptures say, 'In your anger do not sin'[14] and thereby clearly show that anger itself is not innately evil.

Jesus displayed anger; a righteous anger that was vented upon those who had turned the temple, a house of prayer, into a den of thieves. In righteous wrath He made a whip of cords and drove out those who had stoked His fury.

I am angry when I stand beside the hospital bed of someone whose body is being devoured by cancer; angry at the Enemy that through the curse he brought pain and suffering into the world.

Anger becomes right or wrong depending upon its epicentre. When Jesus was angry it was because of that which had polluted His Father's House. Throughout His ministry upon earth, when reviled and spat upon and later crucified, He went as a lamb to the slaughter. He refused to use the weapon of anger in self-defence.

It was Spurgeon who once said, 'When your anger boils over, be careful that it scalds no one but the Devil.'

Jealousy

At the point that God relayed to Moses the moral requirements that He demanded in His people, when furnishing them with the Commandments, He declared Himself to be a jealous God. Later it is recorded that 'They aroused His jealousy with their idols', 'The Lord will be jealous for His land', 'I am jealous for Jerusalem'.[15]

Nor was this trait to be confined to Jehovah who had title deeds to everything and for whom jealousy was justifiable. Paul, as he watched lives with great potential being wasted and given over to godless ends, declares to the church at Corinth, 'I am jealous for you with a godly jealousy'.[16]

Hate

Holiness before God is reached in direct proportion to

the hatred an individual has towards sin. 'To fear the Lord is to hate evil.' 'Hate evil and Love good.' 'Show mercy mixed with fear – hating even the clothing stained by corrupted flesh.'[17]

The righteous reflex of the Christian is to recoil from sin as from a viper. This abhorrence derives its power from an awareness of sin's true nature. It emanates from an understanding of what sin has done to the sinner as well as what sin has done to Christ in making the suffering of Calvary necessary for its removal.

The most positive position for the believer is an escalation in both their love for the sinner and their hatred of sin. Tolerance for sin is only a euphemism for moral anaemia.

Covetousness

God has given the Christian a licence to covet when it comes to eagerly desiring God's highest for our lives. 'Covet eagerly the best gifts'.[18] Paul says to the Corinthians.

Instead of materialistic acquisitiveness we are encouraged to hunger and thirst after righteousness, marshalling all our energies to attain those things that God has prepared for us. We are called upon to stretch our faith to the limit with the goal of acquiring the resources that will bring blessing and release to other people.

It should be noted that in all those areas that we have considered, the one factor that alters the polarity of our passions from negative to positive is the changing of their central focus. It is the Spirit and not the Flesh that produces the activating energy.

Small-mindedness is primarily a problem of focus. It occurs at the point that vision is centred on human inadequacy rather than on divine omnipotence. It values things only as they are and not as they can become.

When the air balloon was invented a sceptic said to Dr Franklin, 'Well it's all very wonderful – but what's the use of it?' He replied, 'What is the use of a new-born infant? The hope is that one day it will become a man.'

Epilogue

Living under the blessing of God, King Solomon prospered. At his death he left behind him a solid gold security system. When Rehoboam came to the throne his reign did not bear the same hallmark of either holiness or wisdom. In consequence he became vulnerable to an incursion of the enemy. 1 Kings 14.25–28 records the following:

> In the fifth year of King Rehoboam, Shishak King of Egypt attacked Jerusalem. He carried off the treasures of the temple of the Lord and the treasures of the royal palace. He took everything, including all the gold shields Solomon had made. So Rehoboam made bronze shields to replace them and assigned these to the commanders of the guard on duty at the entrance to the royal palace. Whenever the king went to the Lord's temple, the guards bore the shields, and afterward they returned them to the guardroom.

The shields were ceremonial, and every time they were displayed before the populace it was immediately apparent that these symbols of defence amounted, in the eyes of the people, to a second-class security system.

Knowing that his time is short, Satan is using every weapon in his arsenal to harangue the Church. God has provided the ultimate defence initiative for the Church but puts the responsibility of covering themselves with it in their hands. Nothing less will do.

Be strong – not in yourselves but in the Lord, in the power of His boundless resource. Put on God's complete armour so that you can successfully resist all the devil's methods of attack. For our fight is not against any physical enemy: it is against organisations and powers that are spiritual. We are up against the unseen power that controls this dark world, and spiritual agents from the very headquarters of evil. Therefore you must wear the whole armour of God that you may be able to resist evil in its day of power, and that even when you have fought to a standstill you may still stand your ground. Take your stand then with truth as your belt, righteousness your breastplate, the gospel of peace firmly on your feet, salvation as your helmet and in your hand the sword of the Spirit, the Word of God. Above all be sure to take faith as your shield, for it can quench every burning missile the enemy hurls at you. Pray at all times with every kind of spiritual prayer, keeping alert and persistent as you pray for all Christ's men and women.

(Ephesians 6.10–18, J.B. Phillips.)

Notes

Chapter 1

1. Proverbs 18.10
2. 1 Corinthians 10.12 (AB)
3. Matthew 26.56
4. Matthew 23.37
5. John 2.1
6. John 20.29
7. John 15.4,7,9; compare also 1 John 2:6,24,28; 3:6,24
8. Psalm 40.2

Chapter 2

1. Genesis 3.9
2. 1 Kings 19.9
3. 1 Kings 17.9
4. Romans 3.25
5. 2 Corinthians 5.17
6. 2 Corinthians 3.18
7. Hebrews 12.15
8. Numbers 11.11; 20.11,12
9. Job 16.12
10. Psalm 10.1
11. Habakkuk 1.2
12. 1 John 1.9
13. Psalm 34.18
14. Job 42.2
15. Habakkuk 3.17–19
16. Proverbs 3.5,6
17. Numbers 2.2
18. Matthew 13.52
19. 1 Kings 19.5

Chapter 3

1. Isaiah 22.22; compare also 36.3
2. Revelation 3.7
3. Revelation 22.16
4. 1 Samuel 17
5. Isaiah 14.15
6. Genesis 1.26–30; compare also Hebrews 2.6–8
7. John 8.34
9. Colossians 2.15
10. Revelation 1.18; 5.5
11. Romans 5.18,19
12. Ephesians 2.6
13. Ephesians 1.20–23
14. Matthew 18.18

Chapter 4

1. 1 Corinthians 10.12
2. Mark 13.13
3. *Mr Jones, Meet The Master*, New York: Fleming H. Revell Company, 1951
4. Proverbs 4.23
5. Matthew 5.27–29
6. Richard Baxter, *The Reformed Pastor*, Puritan Paperbacks, p. 208
7. 1 Corinthians 11.28
8. Psalm 84.11; James 5.16; John 15.7

9. Colossians 3.2; Hebrews 11.1, (J.B. Phillips)
10. Ephesians 6.10–18; Isaiah 4.17; 1 Corinthians 10.13
11. Deuteronomy 1.28
12. Psalm 3.3
13. Genesis 3.1–5
14. John 11.21
15. Romans 16.7
16. Psalm 5.11,12; compare Psalm 18.2
17. Matthew 13.22
18. Psalm 125.1,2
19. Proverbs 30.5
20. Philippians 4.5,6
21. Isaiah 26.1,3
22. Rhona Prime, *Time of Trial*, Hodder and Stoughton
23. 1 John 4.18
24. Job 16.20

Chapter 5

1. Hebrews 12.1 (KJV)
2. Acts 4.13
3. Acts 4.29
4. John 1.33
5. Acts 1.4–8
6. Acts 4.31
7. 1 Samuel 3.1
8. Hebrews 10:19–22
9. 1 Timothy 1.5
10. Proverbs 28.1
11. 1 Peter 3.16; 1 John 3.21 (AB)
12. John 13.6–8; Matthew 16.22; Acts 10.14
13. Matthew 16.23
14. Matthew 26.35
15. Exodus 1.7,11,12
16. Psalm 24.3,4
17. Joshua 9.1,2
18. Revelation 3.11
19. 2 Samuel 5.10,17
20. Genesis 15.1,11
21. Nehemiah 2.17,11; 4:1,7–10
22. Exodus 17.4
23. Song of Songs 2.4
24. Psalm 60.4
25. Romans 11.22
26. Isaiah 13.2–5
27. Isaiah 59.19 (KJV)

Chapter 6

1. Matthew 12.36 (KJV)
2. Speech in the House of Commons, 23 March 1933
3. Ecclesiastes 5.1–6
4. James 3.5–8
5. Psalm 141.3
6. C.H. Spurgeon, *Lectures to my Students*
7. Hebrews 12.15
8. Proverbs 13.3; compare also 18.8,21; 20.19; 21.23; 26.20
9. 1 Corinthians 13.4–7
10. Romans 12.14–21
11. Colossians 2.10 (KJV)
12. Matthew 5.27
13. Leonard Ravenhill, *Sodom Had No Bible*, Bethany House, p. 69
14. Isaiah 53.7

Chapter 7

1. Leviticus 19.18; Matthew 19.19
2. Proverbs 23.7 (KJV)
3. 1 Samuel 18.14
4. John 15.13
5. Mark 10.43
6. Romans 1.14 (KJV)
7. 1 Peter 2.9
8. Ephesians 1.4
9. Acts 3.1–10
10. Revelation 1.18
11. Exodus 3.14
12. Esther 4.14
13. Hebrews 10.10; 1 Timothy 2.5
14. Philippians 2.12,13
15. John 15.5
16. Ephesians 1.13 (KJV); Isaiah 53.3
17. Titus 1.1,10,16
18. John 15.16
19. Psalm 1.3; Genesis 49.22; Mark 11.20
20. 2 Samuel 1.19
21. 1 Corinthians 10.12
22. Psalm 37.23,24
23. Philippians 3.12 (J.B. Phillips)
24. Galatians 3.26–28
25. 2 Corinthians 2.16;3.5,6
26. Philippians 4.13
27. Psalm 2.4; 37.13; 59.8
28. Proverbs 6.6–8
29. Psalm 119.9,11
30. Psalm 104.18; 61.2–4
31. Joel 2.8
32. James 1.8
33. Psalm 67.6
34. 1 Thessalonians 1.3
35. Proverbs 29.25
36. Hebrews 12.2,3

Chapter 8

1. 1 Corinthians 2.9,10
2. Ephesians 3.17–21
3. Joe Haines, *Maxwell*, Guild Publishing, p. 1, 1988
4. Marcus Sieff,*Don't Ask The Price*, Fontana Books, pp. 18, 247
5. Luke 16.8
6. Eric Clark,*The Want Makers*, Hodder and Stoughton, p. 337
7. Mark 10.35–38,46–52
8. Tom Peters,*Thriving on Chaos*, Macmillan, pp. 391, 394, 401
9. Johnson Oatman Jnr and Ada R. Habershon, *Redemption Hymnal*, Hymn 393
10. Deuteronomy 1.6,8
11. Acts 22.105
12. Galatians 1.23
13. Acts 8.3; 20.20
14. Psalm 4.4; Ephesians 4.26
15. Exodus 20.5; Psalm 78.58; Joel 2.18; Zachariah 1.14
16. 2 Corinthians 11.2
17. Proverbs 8.13; Amos 5.15; Jude 23
18. 1 Corinthians 12.31 (KJV)